FROM
INPUT
TO
OUTPUT

A Teacher's Guide to Second
Language Acquisition

The McGraw-Hill Second Language Professional Series

General Editors: James F. Lee and Bill VanPatten

Directions in Second Language Learning

Primarily for students of second language acquisition and teaching, curriculum developers, and teacher educators, *Directions in Second Language Learning* explores how languages are learned and used and how knowledge about language acquisition and use informs language teaching. The books in this strand emphasize principled approaches to language classroom instruction and management as well as to the education of foreign and second language teachers.

From Input to Output: A Teacher's Guide to Second Language Acquisition
by Bill VanPatten (The University of Illinois at Chicago), ISBN 0-07-282561-8
Making Communicative Language Teaching Happen, Second Edition
by James F. Lee (Indiana University) and Bill VanPatten (The University of Illinois at Chicago), ISBN 0-07-365517-1
Translation Teaching: From Research to the Classroom
by Sonia Colina (Arizona State University), ISBN 0-07-248709-7
Gender in the Language Classroom
by Monika Chavez (University of Wisconsin-Madison), ISBN 0-07-236749-0
Tasks and Communicating in Language Classrooms
by James F. Lee (Indiana University), ISBN 0-07-231054-5
Affect in Foreign Language and Second Language Learning: A Practical Guide to Creating a Low-Anxiety Classroom Atmosphere
Edited by Dolly Jesusita Young (The University of Tennessee), ISBN 0-07-038900-4
Communicative Competence: Theory and Classroom Practice, Second Edition
by Sandra J. Savignon (The Pennsylvania State University), ISBN 0-07-083736-8
Beyond Methods: Components of Second Language Teacher Education
Edited by Kathleen Bardovi-Harlig and Beverly Hartford (both of Indiana University), ISBN 0-07-006106-8

Perspectives on Theory and Research

Primarily for scholars and researchers of second language acquisition and teaching, *Perspectives on Theory and Research* seeks to advance knowledge about the nature of language learning in and out of the classroom by offering current research on language learning and teaching from diverse perspectives and frameworks.

Breaking Tradition: An Exploration of the Historical Relationship between Theory and Practice in Second Language Teaching
by Diane Musumeci (University of Illinois, Urbana-Champaign), ISBN 0-07-044394-7

FROM INPUT

TO

OUTPUT

A Teacher's Guide to Second Language Acquisition

Bill VanPatten

The University of Illinois at Chicago

Boston Burr Ridge, IL Dubuque, IA Madison, WI New York
San Francisco St. Louis Bangkok Bogotá Caracas Kuala Lumpur
Lisbon London Madrid Mexico City Milan Montreal New Delhi
Santiago Seoul Singapore Sydney Taipei Toronto

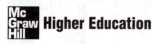

This is an ⌐BⅠ book.

From Input to Output: A Teacher's Guide to Second Language Acquisition

1 2 3 4 5 6 7 8 9 0 BKM BKM 0 9 8 7 6 5 4 3 2

ISBN 0-07-282561-8

Editor-in-chief: *Thailia Dorwick*
Publisher: *William R. Glass*
Development editor: *Kate Engelberg*
Marketing manager: *Nick Agnew*
Project manager: *Jennifer Chambliss*
Senior production supervisor: *Richard DeVitto*
Design manager: *Violeta Díaz*
Cover designer: *Violeta Díaz*
Interior designer: *Linda Robertson*
Art editor: *Cristin Yancey*
Compositor: *Graphic Arts Center*
Typeface: *Times Roman*
Printer: *Bookmart Press, Inc.*

Library of Congress Cataloging-in-Publication Data

VanPatten, Bill.
    From input to output : a teacher's guide to second language acquisition / Bill VanPatten.
        p. cm. – (The McGraw-Hill second language professional series. Directions in second
        language learning)
    Includes bibliographical references and index.
    ISBN 0-07-282561-8
    1. Second language acquisition. 2. Language and languages--Study and teaching. I.
    Title. II. Series.

    P118.2.V36 2002
    418'.0071—dc21

                                                                                    2002035767

http://www.mhhe.com

For all my students and
colleagues in SLA

CONTENTS

How do people acquire another language? If a random person walking down a street were asked this question, a likely answer would be something as simple as, "You learn by practicing" or "Go to another country and live there." But the field of second language acquisition has found that learning another language is far from simple. Most researchers would say that second language acquisition is complex and multifaceted and involves numerous factors too difficult to explain in a one- or two-sentence answer. And as the evidence from all the research since the early 1970s would suggest, second language acquisition is indeed no simple affair.

In this book, Bill VanPatten synthesizes the research on second language acquisition and, importantly, distills it for the nonspecialist. Dispelling a good number of myths, VanPatten presents the reader with concepts from linguistics, psychology, and psycholinguistics in a nontechnical way. He distinguishes, for example, between language use as skill (and how a skill must develop) and language as an underlying competence (and how competence is acquired). He also distinguishes among the processes by which learners gain linguistic data from their environment, the processes by which those data are incorporated into an underlying system, and the processes by which speech processing and skill emerge and develop. In the next to final chapter, he draws on his considerable experiences as a researcher, conference presenter, workshop organizer, and professor to address questions frequently asked by teachers. In short, he peels back the complexity of second language acquisition research and theory to reveal some basic notions that teachers and administrators should have about the learning of another language, especially if they make decisions about curricula and/or evaluate the expected outcomes of those curricula.

The resulting book is easily readable by teachers, administrators, students, and even the layperson—anyone who wants to know how second languages are acquired. The book reflects VanPatten's long-term commitment to making theory and research accessible to nonspecialists. It also reflects his ability to pass back and forth between theory and practice, between research findings and their classroom implications and applications. Well known for his insightful work on input processing and its implications for language instruction, VanPatten goes beyond his previous work and synthesizes in one volume different strands of second language research to reveal the bigger picture. The book makes clear why VanPatten has received so many awards and accolades throughout his teaching career. His enthusiasm for the field of second language research, his ability to predict which constructs and ideas may need definition and explication, his ability to push readers to keep particular constructs in mind as they read, and his now-and-then touch of humor are evidence of why his teaching has received the attention it has.

As Bill VanPatten's frequent co-author, I am uniquely positioned to state that this book is among his best work. I am reminded of one reviewer's comment on the proposal and sample chapter for this book: "If this book were available next term, I would eagerly adopt it for my methods course." This book is the one around which those of us in language departments can build our offerings in Applied Linguistics.

In the tradition of the various books in the McGraw-Hill Second Language Professional Series—which strives to pull together theory, research, and practice— VanPatten's book is a welcome and needed addition.

James F. Lee
Bloomington, IN
September 26, 2002

This book is about second language acquisition. My reasons for writing a short book about a complex human endeavor boil down to three. One is that my colleagues in literary studies sometimes ask me where they can read something nontechnical, not too dense, and completely up-to-date in second language acquisition. Many of these colleagues know virtually nothing about linguistics, psycholinguistics, or language acquisition and hold beliefs that run counter to all current research and theory. Perhaps the most recent motivation to write this book came from my department head, Christopher Maurer. He said to me, "Bill, what I need is a short, concise book so that I can understand what it is you and others are about." I started this book not too long after he said that.

My second reason stems from my having worked in teacher education for some fifteen years and in language program direction for the other five years of my career. Undergraduates pursuing certification in language teaching often get one and only one course in so-called "methods," as do graduate teaching assistants. In spite of my belief that this is simply wrong—that is, if you are going to teach language, you'd better know a lot about language and a lot about how it is learned—I recognize that teacher education students may have time only for a "crash course" in second language acquisition. This crash course needs to expose them to as much as we know about second language acquisition without burdening an already crowded course on language teaching. Like my colleagues in literary studies, they need a brief, readable, and accessible text. Standard texts used to introduce graduate students to second language acquisition are simply too dense, too technical, and too thorough—albeit rightly so on all accounts for their intended audience.

My third reason has to do with the fact that my work is in second language acquisition in a foreign language context. Although I do not believe that languages are acquired differently in different contexts, people who teach in the foreign language context like to hear from their own. Books written by my colleagues in ESL are viewed skeptically at times because they say, "ESL is different from foreign languages." I thus wanted to see a book that could speak to both ESL and foreign language teachers. Since no one else in foreign languages stepped up to the plate, I thought, "Why not me?"

As I began to envision a short book on second language acquisition, however, I realized that I needed to talk about second language acquisition in a way that was different from the "standard" account. That is, rather than discuss second language acquisition broadly in terms of topics and themes, I needed to talk about it in terms of processes and products. In my thinking, we need to start with input and figure out both how learners end up with a linguistic system and how they tap that system to make output. Then we need to look at the myriad factors related to the processes that connect all these products and how they, too, are interconnected. This approach is quite different from discussing the nature of interlanguage, learner output, research methods, theories, first language vs. second language acquisition, and other themes that tend to dominate graduate-level texts. I also wanted to include my thoughts on both input and output because, given that I research the role of input and input processing in language acquisition, some people have assumed that output plays no role. I hope this book puts that notion to rest.

If I have achieved my goals, then this book should be

- a short and concise text (useful as a supplement in methods courses);
- a reader-friendly text (with little jargon and clear definitions when needed);
- a way to put different aspects of language acquisition into perspective.

The book can be used in several ways (and I myself have used the manuscript in these ways):

- as part of graduate teaching assistant orientation (it's short enough that major points can be covered in an hour a day over a full week);
- as a supplement to a methods course;
- as the main text in an extension course for public school teachers (with articles and other readings as the supplements and spin-offs).

ORGANIZATION AND FEATURES

The text is organized into five chapters plus a substantive introductory chapter and a substantive epilogue. The Introduction provides basic information on the scope and background of contemporary SLA research. It also lays out the plan of the book for students. Chapter 1 presents some "givens" about SLA—five important findings of SLA research that comprise the basic understandings in the field today. Chapters 2, 3, and 4 cover the major parts of the SLA process—input (Chapter 2), the developing system (Chapter 3), and output (Chapter 4). Each chapter describes and discusses what is currently known about these processes. Chapter 5 offers answers to frequently asked questions—questions that language teachers and students of SLA are most likely to have. Finally, the epilogue describes the implications of SLA research for teaching, showing how the principles derived from research can be applied in the classroom and providing some practical guidelines and sample lessons.

Following the model set in *Making Communicative Language Teaching Happen*, the book Jim Lee and I wrote in 1995 to launch this series, I have included "Pause to Consider. . ." boxes throughout the text. These "think about it" boxes are strategically placed to get the reader to consider what he or she has just read and to develop ideas a bit further. The boxes are designed to invite more thoughtful reflection before the reader continues. I have found them to be quite successful and have used them in the following ways:

- as discussion questions for students to prepare before coming to class;
- as writing assignments;
- as topics for individual presentations in class.

To help students understand the most important concepts in SLA, I have identified key terms in each chapter. They are printed in boldface type and clearly defined in context. They also appear in a comprehensive glossary at the end of the book.

Each chapter ends with a list of further readings entitled "Read More about It." These listings really serve two functions. First, they include the readings upon which the chapter is based. I know that constant in-text citation can get in the way of reading for some students. In an effort to keep the text readable and accessible, I have opted not to include rigorous documentation within chapter narratives and instead to include my sources in these listings. This may not seem "scholarly" to some, but my intent was not to write a scholarly book. My goal, again, was to provide the nonexpert with an introduction to second language acquisition. The second function of the "Read More about It" listings is as a starting point for those students who want to know more about SLA. They can find here a range of books and articles for further reading; more challenging readings have been indicated with an icon.

ACKNOWLEDGMENTS

I am grateful to a number of people who read the manuscript and gave me feedback while it was in development. My first thanks go to Joe Barcoft, Christopher Maurer, and Wynne Wong, who read the earliest version. Thanks are also due to the four outside readers who examined the proposal and Chapter 1 as part of McGraw-Hill's review process. They are Frank B. Brooks, Florida State University; Susan Gass, Michigan State University; Edwin M. Lamboy, Montclair State University; and Gayle Vierma, University of Southern California. Their very positive response as well as their questions and concerns were important in developing the final version of this book. Thanks are due to Paola "Giuli" Dussias, too, who read the proposal and synopsis of chapters and provided initial feedback independently of the review process. Extra special thanks go to my colleagues at The University of Illinois at Chicago, Elliott Judd and Jessica Williams. Their meticulous reading of the entire manuscript provided me with excellent feedback. (It's wonderful when you have great colleagues to work with!) I also need to thank Pat Langley, whose voice in my graduate methods class reminded me that concepts and jargon get in the way of understanding concepts. Her reading of the manuscript resulted in a better product. Mark Overstreet also did a careful reading of the final draft and provided me with many good suggestions and corrections. He was such a great assistant director that I was able to spend time at home working on the manuscript. I need to thank Susanne Rott for keeping my spirits up and encouraging me to do this book. Our team teaching of the "methods course" allowed me to sit back at times and observe student needs. I hope those needs are addressed in this book. I am also grateful for the feedback provided by students in Frank Brooks' and Jean-Louis Dassier's summer 2002 course at the University of Southern Mississippi. Mary Catherine Clarkson, Yoshitaka Fujii, Andrea Garberina, Kristy Glenn, Dawn Hager, Ted Hovorka, Aasya Waheed Malik, Michael McGill, Mary Ellen Radloff, Judith Ann Rene, Melanie Reynolds, Anne Reynolds-Case, Kira Salisbury, Lise Stevens, and Alec Valentine.

Thanks are also due to William R. Glass, my publisher, and all the folks at McGraw-Hill who made this book happen, especially Kate Engelberg, my editor. She was simply terrific to work with. I would also like to thank the Editorial, Design, and Production team who assisted with this book: Jennifer Chambliss, Richard Devitto, Violeta Díaz, and Cristin Yancey.

I would also like to thank a number of people in the field who have inspired me over the years and whom I hold in the greatest of admiration. They had nothing directly to do with this book, but they have been a real presence in my mind throughout my career: Roger Andersen, Robert Bley-Vroman, Craig Chaudron, Susan Gass, Steve Krashen, Patsy Lightbown, Mike Long, Dick Schmidt, Nina Spada, Merrill Swain, Tracy Terrell, and Lydia White. My final thanks to Jim Lee for his continued support not only on this project but on others as well. He's a great colleague and a true friend. Where would we be without people to help us?

Bill VanPatten
Chicago, September 30, 2002

Introduction

Teachers often come to **second language acquisition (SLA)** research looking for concrete answers to teaching questions. If you are an instructor, you might ask questions such as, "What's the best way to correct compositions?", "How do you teach the subjunctive effectively?", and more broadly, "What's the best method for teaching and learning languages?" These are very valid questions for teachers. Unfortunately for teachers, they are not the questions that are addressed in SLA research; teachers may have great expectations for the research that simply aren't its goal. This is not to say that SLA theory and research don't have implications for teaching; they do. But one should not come to SLA research for answers to questions about day-to-day matters of teaching and testing. So why should teachers read this book? Why should teachers—or anyone—study SLA?

THE SCOPE OF SLA RESEARCH

To answer these questions, let's first describe what SLA research is and what its purpose is. Research in SLA attempts to answer the fundamental question, "How does **acquisition** of a second language occur—that is, how do learners of a native language internalize the linguistic system of another language?" (Technically there is also such a thing as third language acquisition—and fourth and fifth language acquisition—but most researchers tend to look only at the acquisition of a second language.) This basic question spawns a number of smaller questions:

- What do learners do when acquiring another language?
- What stages do they go through?
- What does their second language look like?
- What kinds of errors do they make?
- What factors affect acquisition?

Over the years, the fundamental question has been broadened to include not only an internal linguistic system but also the "mechanisms" that make use of that system. So, another question that some in SLA explore is, "How do learners access and make use of this internalized linguistic system to communicate?" This question in turn involves a number of its own subquestions:

- What are the mechanisms learners use to produce language?
- Are errors that learners produce errors in their linguistic system or errors related to the mechanisms they use to produce language?
- How does fluency develop?

In a sense, all of these questions are much more basic than those that teachers often ask. We say "more basic" because a question such as, "What's the best way to correct compositions?" assumes that error correction does something. Questions such as, "How do you teach the subjunctive effectively?" assume there is a relationship between teaching efforts and acquisition. Again, teachers have a right to ask such questions since this is the stuff of their daily existence. What SLA theorists and researchers study and labor at, however, is not teaching but learning. One question that SLA research should ultimately be able to address for all teachers is this: "Which instructional efforts actually further acquisition and which do not?" What SLA seeks to find out about, then, are the processes and products of acquisition independent of context (for example, whether teaching is involved or not). Over the years, SLA research has increasingly moved away from classroom issues; that change is good for SLA research but not helpful for teachers asking the kinds of questions mentioned earlier. Not to despair, however; there are some matters that SLA can already speak to regarding instructional efforts. But more on that later in this book.

THE ORIGINS OF CONTEMPORARY SLA RESEARCH

Contemporary SLA research got its start when two separate intellectual pursuits coalesced. One was related to language teaching, the other to child first language acquisition (in turn as a result of the influential writings of Noam Chomsky). The first of these threads began in the 1950s and 1960s, when behaviorism dominated the field of psychology. **Behaviorism** was a theory associated with Pavlov and his salivating dogs but popularized by the work of B. F. Skinner. In this paradigm, all learning could be "reduced" to what was called operant conditioning. Basically this means that given X, Y happens. Learners learn to do Y because they are rewarded when X is present. Pavlov gave his dogs treats while ringing a bell (X). Giving them treats made them salivate (Y) in anticipation of the treats. The dogs began to associate bells with treats and hence the bells (X) induced salivation (Y). Skinner extended this line of thinking and research into various realms of human behavior, including linguistic behavior. Skinner said that learning a language was like learning anything else; we are rewarded when we do it right and that causes us to learn. Reward may come in the form of praise or in the form of communicative success.

In response to World War II and the Cold War, the U.S. armed forces developed the Army Method of language instruction, borrowing language descriptions from structural linguistics (the dominant way of analyzing language at the time) and fashioning their own interpretation of operant conditioning: language drilling. (This was the army; if you could drill other behaviors, why not drill language?) Learners imitated, repeated, performed operations on the sentences they heard, and were "rewarded" for their correct display of language behavior, that is, not making errors. Given the raging Cold War, significant funds were diverted to nonmilitary sources for developing effective ways to teach languages. The result was a widespread diffusion of the Army Method (renamed the **Audiolingual Method,** or audiolingualism, and nicknamed **ALM**) into academic circles, both secondary and postsecondary, in the late 1950s and 1960s. The basic tenets of ALM were that language consisted of a set of habits, that first language habits interfered with learning the habits of the second language and had to be suppressed, and that errors were to be avoided during production and when they did occur, they were to be corrected imme- *ALM* diately with the proper habit imitated by the learner. In ALM classes, then, learners memorized dialogues, rehearsed language during drills, and so on. Spontaneous speech was avoided because this would induce errors and cause problems in the learning of the correct habits.

At about the same time that ALM reached its zenith, research on child first language acquisition began to appear, forming the second thread in the development of contemporary SLA research. In the early to mid-1960s, empirical data emerged that seriously challenged the behaviorist account of what children do. Children were seen to be "creators" of linguistic systems and not mere parrots who mimicked and repeated after their caregivers. Children, regardless of socioeconomic status or geographic location, evidenced strikingly similar if not identical patterns of errors and development in their first language. For example, children acquired a certain set of fourteen verb and noun inflections (such as past tense marking, third-person –s, progressive, possessive, and others) as well as certain "functors" (such as articles and linking verbs) in an order that was invariant across children studied. As another example, children went through strikingly similar stages of development in their acquisition of structures and rules such as question formation and negation, among others. (In subsequent chapters we will see something quite similar for L2 learners). In addition, it was shown that errors that were certainly possible during acquisition never occurred. Eventually, first language acquisition was seen as the intersection of two important factors: internal mechanisms the child is born with and the language data the child is exposed to in everyday interactions (what is called the *input*.) Chomsky challenged Skinner's ideas as far back as the mid-1950s; he underscored the creative nature of language and pointed out that children couldn't possibly learn from imitation and repetition alone. (As we will see in Chapters 1 and 3, you, as a speaker of a language, know and can do far more with language than what you have been exposed to over the years.) Chomsky demonstrated how a grammar of a language is generative, meaning ✗ that you could generate an infinite number of sentences from a finite set of rules. For example, by knowing the rules for plural formation, you can pluralize any noun that is pluralizable. This contrasted with the concept of imitation and repetition by which, theoretically, you could produce only that which you had heard in the past. Chomsky also demonstrated that native speakers of a language can judge sentences to be ungrammatical or impossible structures when they can't have learned the rule based on exemplars in the input, that is, the language they'd been exposed to all their lives.

How do we account for these phenomena? According to Chomsky, we can account for them only if language is a special part of human behavior and knowledge. As a species, we are born with the capacity to make language; it is part of our genetic makeup. We are literally born with genetic information that *shapes and constrains* what we can do with language. This is what allows us to learn languages so quickly as children and also allows us to know more than what we could by mere exposure to the linguistic data that surround us. (You will see plenty of examples of this concept in Chapter 1 as well as in Chapter 3.)

Some people who were involved in second language teaching read these accounts of child language acquisition and began questioning both language teaching practices and the psychological theory that underlay them, namely, behaviorism. In 1967, an influential paper was published in the *International Review of Applied Linguistics* that probably marks the onset of contemporary SLA research. That paper was written by S. Pit Corder and was titled, "The significance of learners' errors." In that paper, Corder argues that rather than see errors as problematic, perhaps the profession should study them as windows into the learning process. He explains that errors may reveal systematic patterns of behavior that in turn reflect underlying processes that behaviorism could never account for. He made the following very important and powerful point as the conclusion of his paper:

> We have been reminded recently of von Humboldt's statement that we cannot really teach language, we can only create conditions in which it will develop spontaneously in the mind in its own way. We shall never improve our ability to create such favorable conditions until we learn more about the way a learner learns and what his built-in syllabus is. When we do know this (and the learner's errors will, if systematically studied, tell us something about this) we may begin to be more critical of our cherished notions. We may be able to allow the learner's innate strategies to dictate our practice and determine our syllabus; we may learn to adapt ourselves to *his* needs rather than impose upon him *our* preconceptions of *how* he ought to learn, *what* he ought to learn and *when* he ought to learn it. (Corder, 1967, reprinted in Corder, 1981, pp. 12–13, emphasis original)

Not long after the publication of Corder's paper, additional theoretical and empirical work in SLA began to appear. Pioneering work was published by Heidi Dulay and Marina Burt, Kenji Hakuta, Evelyn Hatch, Steve Krashen, Diane Larsen-Freeman, John Schumann, Larry Selinker, Merrill Swain, Henning Wode, and many others in the early and mid-1970s. For the first time in any discussions related to language acquisition and language teaching, descriptive and experimental evidence about SLA was finally available. A good deal of it showed the creative process by which second language learners "reconstructed" the grammar of the second language (a point we take up in Chapter 1). All the cherished beliefs about SLA began to crumble, and the field has never been the same since.

Corder's statement, then, provides the answer to the question, "Why should teachers study SLA?" The more you know about SLA (its processes and products), the better you can gauge what instructional efforts are worth your while and what method or methods work best for teaching and learning languages. To put this another way, basic knowledge of how acquisition happens is fundamental to ones' education and training as a language teacher; if you are trying to make a difference, you need to know what you are making a difference in. Some people might say, however, that as classroom teachers what you really need to know about are insights from cognitive psychology and educational psychology about how people learn in general, that is, how they process information, organize it, store it, and use it. Although there is rationale for knowing something about learning in general, an underlying position in this book that surfaces now and then is the same as Chomsky's, Corder's, and others': There is something special about language, and even for second language learners, acquisition may not obey general principles of learning alone. In other words, language acquisition—whether first or second—involves processes and mechanisms that are unique to language.

SOME CAVEATS

This book is organized differently from books for graduate students pursuing research careers in SLA and from other "short course" books on SLA (to my knowledge, there are only two others). Most books present research findings around topics or themes. Typical themes are theories of SLA, the linguistic environment, the role of the first language, nature versus nurture, research methods used, and individual differences, among others. This book is not organized around these themes, though they do show up in one way or another as part of the discussion. Instead, this book is organized around three fundamental components of SLA and the processes that are used with them: input, the developing system, and output. For me, organizing the book this way helps to bring the different strands of research and different theoretical approaches together in a more cohesive way. My perspective is that not all theories compete for explanation, but they actually explain different things. (Some do compete for explanation, and this is indicated where necessary.) My goal is to help you develop a sense of the processes involved in SLA and an appreciation of the complexity of the task that faces every language learner.

This book takes an almost exclusively psycholinguistic perspective on acquisition, meaning that it focuses on the internal processes of acquisition and their relationships to the products of acquisition. Psycholinguists, in general, do not study linguistic systems per se—that is, they don't attempt to come up with a description of the organization of the linguistic system. Instead, psycholinguists focus on how a linguistic system is used and what factors affect that use. They ask questions such as, "How do people interpret sentences when there is ambiguity?", "Under what conditions do the mechanisms responsible for comprehending an utterance break down and fail to produce comprehension?", "How do people produce utterances?", and many others. To underscore, these questions all reflect processes and mechanisms used to either comprehend or produce language. This book takes that same perspective, focusing on the processes and internal factors that affect how learners develop a linguistic system.

To be sure, there are other approaches to studying SLA; three of them tend to predominate (in addition to the psycholinguistic). In the purely *linguistic approach*, researchers use a particular linguistic theory to see if they can explain what constrains the development of the learner's linguistic system, if it is constrained at all. The *cognitive approaches* apply certain theories from cognitive psychology (that is, general learning theories and not language learning theories specifically) to account for the development of the learner's linguistic system. The *sociocultural approaches* focus on the contexts in which language acquisition happens, specifically, interactional contexts (between teacher and learner or learner and learner, for example). The attempt in sociocultural approaches is to understand the purpose and intent underlying the interactions in order to explain learning in general. If you continue any work in SLA, you will surely encounter these approaches and at that point can determine to what extent you agree with them.

The approach taken in this book is not meant as a rejection of these different approaches or any others. In fact, many aspects of these approaches are incorporated into the larger picture developed over the course of this book. The process approach taken here—centered around input, the developing system, and output—helps to bring various strands of research together. Admittedly, the perspective here is mine, and in an attempt to simplify concepts, state them clearly, and unify them into an overall picture of SLA, I may not have done justice to the field of SLA research as a whole. This is always a risk one takes when attempting a book such as this; my hope is that my colleagues in the field of SLA will understand the intent of my presentation and forgive any omissions. But I also believe that most scholars in SLA will agree with a good deal of the content of this book and find it to be mainstream in nature.

One final caveat is that the focus of this book is the development of a linguistic system. The fundamental question to be addressed is, "How do learners create a linguistic system that underlies language use?" Thus, issues related to the development of literacy will not be reviewed here. Reading, comprehension of written texts, and composition of written texts lie outside the scope of this short book.

ORGANIZATION OF THE BOOK

Before examining the processes and products of SLA, the first chapter gives a quick overview of some accepted findings or conclusions from the research. Only five are presented. There are more, but if we included more, we might as well have you read one of the expert-oriented works on SLA instead, the kind intended for doctoral students of SLA. The reason for limiting the findings presented in the first chapter is to quickly orient you to some of the topics and to jump-start you into the discussion of the processes and products. But don't worry, you aren't being shortchanged; other findings and important topics appear throughout the book, especially in Chapters 2 (on input), 3 (on the developing system), and 4 (on output). Chapter 5 contains frequently asked questions and their answers. And because I *do* think that SLA research can speak to language teaching in certain ways, the Epilogue includes implications for language teaching. These implications are not exhaustive but are suggestive of the nature of curricula that foster SLA in classrooms. They should be taken as guidelines with which instructors can begin to explore the many options that exist in language teaching today; they may also be used as yardsticks by which to measure textbooks and materials available to instructors.

If you know nothing about SLA formally, that is, if you have not read any work on SLA at all, some aspects of SLA discussed in this book may surprise you. I encourage you to note this when it does happen. Keep a notebook next to you as you read, and every time you are surprised or learn something that goes against what you thought you knew, jot it down. You might discern a pattern to your thinking that is worth reflecting on. On the other hand, some of you may find that the discussions in this book support some of your common-sense notions or experiences you have had in teaching and learning languages. Whatever your particular situation, if this is the first time you are reading about SLA, be prepared for some challenges! If you are currently teaching, you may want to share some ideas with your students to see how they react. Knowing about acquisition as opposed to relying on common beliefs may help learners understand certain nontraditional curricula they are experiencing.

So, let's not wait any longer. Turn the page to begin reading about some givens in SLA theory and research. *Bonne lecture!*

READ MORE ABOUT IT

Corder, S. P. (1981). *Error analysis and interlanguage*. Oxford: Oxford University Press. (Reprinted from Corder, S. P. (1967). The significance of learners' errors. *International Review of Applied Linguistics, 5*, 161–170.)

Hatch, E. M. (1978). *Second language acquisition: A book of readings*. Rowley, MA: Newbury House. [This book in particular contains early empirical research mentioned in this chapter, conducted by Dulay and Burt, Krashen, Schuman, Wode, and others.]

Krashen, S. D. (1981). *Second language acquisition and second language learning*. New York: Pergamon.

Lightbown, P. (1985). Great expectations: Second language acquisition research and classroom teaching. *Applied Linguistics, 6*, 173–189.

Mitchell, R., & Myles, F. (1998). *Second language learning theories*. London: Arnold.

Selinker, L. (1972). Interlanguage. *International Review of Applied Linguistics, 10*, 209–231.

CHAPTER 1

Some Givens about Second Language Acquisition

Like the natural sciences and social sciences, SLA—or better yet, how we conceptualize SLA—is an area of study built upon empirical research. Researchers in SLA either gather descriptive data (e.g., by asking questions such as, "What does the speech of an intermediate learner of French with English as a first language look like?") or test hypotheses derived from some kind of theorizing (e.g., "Based on a theory of linguistics, structure A should be more difficult than structure B for learners. I'll research this by recording whether learners make more errors with A than they do with B.") So, researchers in SLA have gathered observations and facts over the years, just as researchers in the natural sciences and social sciences have.

From these observations and facts we can fashion certain statements about SLA in general, that is, regardless of the context of learning. In the present discussion, **context of learning** refers to the environment in which languages are learned. There are two main determinants of context: (1) whether the language is spoken in the country where the learning is taking place and (2) whether any classroom experience is involved. In a **foreign language context,** the language is not normally spoken outside of the classroom, as would be the case in learning French in Iowa City. In a **second language context,** the language is spoken in the country or area where it is being learned. This context includes English in the United States or Australia, French in Quebec, and so on. A second language context may also be differentiated by whether there is instruction or not. A person might be learning French in an intensive language program in Quebec City and also find herself immersed in the language upon leaving the classroom. On the other hand, a person might emigrate to the United States and for various reasons not take any classes but pick up English from interactions with natives. In this book and in the field of SLA in general, a **second language** (often abbreviated L2) is any language other than the person's first language (L1). So, for that learner of French in Iowa City, the field of SLA research would say that French is a second language being learned in a foreign language context.

When we say, then, that we can make statements about SLA in general regardless of context, we mean that *the observed facts can be found in any context* where a second language is learned. It makes no difference whether the context is a second language environment (where the other language is spoken) or a foreign language environment (where the language is not spoken). It makes no difference whether the context involves a classroom or whether acquisition takes place exclusively or almost exclusively outside of a classroom, such as in the case of immigrants.

Pause to consider . . .

why context would *not* make a difference in learning another language. What kinds of things can you think of that might be part of SLA that are not context-dependent? Do you think learning a foreign language is somehow fundamentally different from learning a second language? That is, do you think that somehow a classroom experience alters or changes whatever mental processes are involved in learning a language? Or do you think that the context affects only the external factors that exist outside the learner's brain?

In this chapter, we review five "givens," or possible statements that can be made, about SLA in general. They are:

1. SLA involves the creation of an implicit (unconscious) linguistic system;
2. SLA is complex and consists of different processes;
3. SLA is dynamic but slow;
4. most L2 learners fall short of native-like competence;
5. skill acquisition is different from the creation of an implicit system.

These five have been selected because of their interest for language teachers (and students as well, for that matter). Some of these statements may seem self-evident; that is, one could say, "You didn't need to do research to tell me that!" Very often in such cases, however, there is more to the statement than meets the eye.

STATEMENT 1: SLA INVOLVES THE CREATION OF AN IMPLICIT (UNCONSCIOUS) LINGUISTIC SYSTEM

All speakers of a first language—or signers if we are dealing with individuals with hearing impairments—have an **implicit linguistic system** in their heads. By *implicit* we mean that the system exists outside of consciousness; you are unaware of its properties even though you may use it every single second of your life. When you say, "Stan, don't forget to pick up the dry cleaning" to someone as he walks out the door, you are not thinking about the system. It's just there. You call upon the rules of grammar, vocabulary, and so forth, without thinking about anything. What is more, you can make declarations about sentences or structures being possible or impossible in your first language without knowing why. A **possible sentence** (or **possible structure**) is one that your native-language grammar allows, even if you wouldn't say it yourself. An impossible sentence is one that your native grammar would rule out. Here's an example. Accepting that the contraction *wanna* is a part of contemporary English, which of these two sentences sounds possible in English and which strikes you as impossible? Careful! Don't read *wanna* as *wanta*.

(1) Who do you wanna invite to the party tonight?
(2) Who do you wanna bring the potato chips to the party tonight?

You probably had an immediate negative reaction to (2)—and you're right. It's not a possible sentence in English, although (1) is.[1] Why isn't it? Unless you thought a lot and conducted lots of analytical work or unless you have a background in theoretical linguistics, you probably would not come up with a satisfactory explanation. You simply *know* that it's a bad sentence. Here's another example at the word level. Look at these pairs of words and then answer the question that follows.

(3) interesting/uninteresting
(4) lawful/unlawful
(5) loyal/disloyal
(6) enchanted/disenchanted

Question: What's the rule for using either *un-* or *dis-* as a prefix to create a word with an opposite meaning?

Again, unless you thought and thought or had a background in linguistics, you probably could not answer the question. Another example is the following: Why is it possible to say *I gave the book to Steve* and *I gave Steve the book* but only *I donated the money to the foundation* and not **I donated the foundation the money*? (Note: We use asterisks in linguistics to denote that a sentence is not a possible sentence in a language.) And just to drive the point home, why do you think (7b) is possible but (7d) is not?

(7a) Who do you think Kate met yesterday?
(7b) Who do you think that Kate met yesterday?
(7c) Who do you think arrived with Kate yesterday?
(7d) *Who do you think that arrived with Kate yesterday?

By now you are probably asking yourself, "Just what are the rules involved in all these examples?" Unfortunately, the rules of theoretical linguistics are not simple ones like "verbs must agree with their subjects." They involve highly abstract concepts that would require a good deal of time to simplify and explain here. Fortunately, you don't need to know the rules because you *already* know them; you just can't verbalize them. They exist outside your awareness and are part of your implicit linguistic system. Of course, some things you do know because you were explicitly taught or you learned them in school. These tend to be rules of usage tied into "good behavior with language" or "appropriateness." Examples of these include (for some speakers of English, not all people!):

---

[1]The correct sentence (2) would be *Who do you want to bring the potato chips to the party?* with no contraction.

- the *who/whom* distinction (*Whom do you like?* is preferable to *Who do you like?*);
- the *that/which* distinction for relative clauses (*The book that I read last night is on the table* is preferable to *The book which I read last night is on the table*);
- the use of a singular pronoun with *everyone* (*Everyone should take his or her book out and look at page 65* is preferable to *Everyone should take their book out. . .*).

There are other similar rules. What is interesting about these rules, by the way, is that they *prescribe what should be done and do not describe what people normally do*. That we can say in English, "Everyone should take *their* books out . . ." or, "The book which I read . . ." means that there are implicit rules that allow us to do this. If it weren't possible, we couldn't do it!

Pause to consider . . .

the difference between what is possible in your language and what teachers may have told you is "the correct way" to express something. Can you think of any other examples of things you know people say or can say in English (or your native language) but that "grammar books" or high school teachers say are not good? Example: double negatives in English—*I don't* (or *ain't*) *got none* versus *I don't have any.*

L2 learners construct similar implicit systems as they go about the task of SLA. This does not mean that they always have implicit systems that match exactly what a native speaker might have (see statement 4), but that is not the point. The point is that whatever system a learner acquires is implicit. How do we know this? By giving them tests just like the ones above about rules they couldn't possibly have learned from textbooks or from teachers.

For example, a colleague and I gathered data on fourth-semester learners of Spanish at the university level. We tested them on certain abstract properties of Spanish grammar that they could not have learned from a book. We also knew that what we tested them on were things we normally do not see as mistakes that learners make, so they couldn't have learned about these through correction. One example is that English allows a construction such as *John has eaten but Mary has not*; Spanish does not allow such constructions; **Juan ha comido pero Marìa no ha* is impossible in Spanish, as is **Juan ha comido pero Marìa ha no*. Spanish must use the full verb phrase, as in *Juan ha comido pero Marìa no ha comido* (John has eaten but Mary has not eaten), or the entire phrase must be deleted, as in *Juan ha comido pero Marìa no* (which sounds odd in English: "John has eaten but Mary not"). Another example is that Spanish allows adverbs between verbs and their direct objects, so that *Marìa ve a menudo la televisión* is possible but its English counterpart is not; **Mary watches often TV* is not a permissible structure. (All these examples are tied to the same abstract property of grammar, which we need not discuss here.) We asked our learners to make **grammaticality judgments,** that is, to tell us whether the Spanish sentences were good/possible or bad/not possible and how they knew. The percentages of judgment types are shown in Table 1.1.

TABLE 1.1 Percentage of Judgment Types for Structures Learners Were Never Taught and Did Not Learn in Class

Judged by Feel	Judged by Using a Known Rule
64	27

Note: All sentences were judged correctly. Subjects = 64 fourth-semester university students of Spanish. From VanPatten and Mandell, 1999.

TABLE 1.2 Percentage of Judgment Types for Structures Learners Were Taught and Had Practiced

Judged by Feel	Judged by Using a Known Rule
27	67

Note: All sentences were judged correctly. Subjects = 64 fourth-semester university students of Spanish. From VanPatten and Mandell, 1999.

As the table shows, the majority of learners couldn't tell us why they judged a sentence the way they did, indicating they did it by feel or some other such manner. Of those who claimed to have judged these by a rule, it is not at all clear they had a rule from class or a textbook. We probed a few students about their rules, and they made the rules up on the spot!

At the same time, we tested these students of Spanish on rules that they had learned and practiced in class, such as the difference between *ser* and *estar* (two linking verbs). Their reasons for judgments are displayed in Table 1.2.

As you can see from Table 1.2, the students felt they knew a rule. Those who were probed could indeed state some kind of rule, albeit not using the language a text or linguist might use. So, by the fourth semester, learners of languages in a classroom situation are already beginning to create an implicit system in their heads. But it is also worth pointing out that second language learners may indeed have **explicit knowledge** or **explicit rules,** especially if they have experienced any classroom language learning. They may know things consciously and be able to express rules in some way—such as verb-subject agreement, the difference between an active and a passive sentence, when to use *du* in French, and so on—just as the learners in our study could articulate something on the two linking verbs *ser* and *estar* in Spanish. They know these things the same way native speakers do; they are taught these rules explicitly, just as native speakers of English may be taught the *who/whom* or *that/which* distinctions. And just as native speakers do, L2 learners store this explicit or explicitly learned information separately from their implicit systems. (It is possible that L1 speakers and L2 speakers come to get such rules in their implicit systems, but as we will argue later, it is not because the learned rule turns into an implicit rule with "practice.") Later in this book, we touch upon the relationship between these explicit and implicit systems and we discuss how fluent users of a language must ultimately rely on an implicit system and not an explicit system.

(handwritten margin notes)
① grammar rules function like a grid or a skeleton on which communication rests
② communication is a sort of game where proper exercise of rules leads to a successful conclusion.

Pause to consider . . .

other explicit rules you have about your language. Why are you given these   rules? What have teachers (or parents) told you regarding these usages?

STATEMENT 2: SLA IS COMPLEX AND CONSISTS OF DIFFERENT PROCESSES

To some people, saying that SLA is complex is like saying that building an airplane is complex. But this statement is not necessarily self-evident to others (including some instructors). Examine the following not so far-fetched things you might hear about SLA.

- "Learning a language all comes down to motivation. You learn if you're motivated; you don't if you're not."
- "If you really want to learn the language, go live where it is spoken and stay with a family that doesn't speak your language."
- "Drills are necessary. That's the way I learned [insert a language here]."
- "Learning is a matter of having a good ear. Some people do and some people don't."
- "Children learn by imitating. Adults learn by studying and practicing."

What's important is not whether these statements are true but how they reduce SLA to one or two simple issues. However, SLA is not simple. The following is a partial list of what a person must acquire (depending on the language type) to learn a second language:

- the **lexicon**—words and their meanings.
- what words can do—For example, some verbs can take an object, like *to hit*, and some cannot, like *to seem*.
- the **phonology**—the sound system, pronunciation.
- inflectional **morphology**—for example, endings on verbs and nouns: *talk, talks, talked; dog, dogs.*
- derivational morphology—the use of prefixes and sometimes suffixes to create new words: *transport, transportation; behave, misbehave.*
- particles—For example, in Japanese certain one-syllable words are tagged onto sentences to indicate a question or some other type of utterance.
- **syntax**—the rules that govern what is a permissible sentence and what is not, such as examples (1) and (2) in the previous section.
- **pragmatics**—what speakers intend by a sentence. For example, in some languages you can make a suggestion by asking a question, as in English. *Why don't you take a break?* is meant to suggest a rest period to someone who looks tired, *Why is SLA so difficult?* is a question to be answered with *Because . . . .*

- **sociolinguistics**—what is appropriate and inappropriate use of language in particular situations; for example, whether to use *tu* or *vous* in French or *Howz it goin?* instead of *Good afternoon* in English.
- **discourse competence**—what makes language cohesive and what is permissible or accepted in a language regarding cohesion across sentences. For example, *Mary ran down the street. John saw her, but didn't say anything* is cohesive, but *Mary ran down the street. He didn't say anything. John did see her* is not, unless you add *though* at the very end, and even then it doesn't sound as good as the other version! Discourse competence also involves such things as turn-taking in a language during conversation.

This list is a reduction and simplification of what needs to be learned. Now, imagine that learning those things *happens all at the same time in SLA*, and you can begin to see just how complex the learning process is when it comes to language. At any given moment, a learner is juggling many if not all of those different aspects of language at once. If we couple this with the fact that learners are engaged in learning how to comprehend language as well as learning how to speak it, we add another layer of complexity.

Pause to consider . . .

what it takes to either understand or produce the following utterances in English: "I think it's chilly in here. Don't you?" How many different aspects of language can you identify in these eight words, using the previous list as a guide?

As we will see in the following chapters, it is not just what has to be learned that is complex; the processes involved in learning it are also complex. At least three distinct sets of processes are involved in language acquisition, all of them going on at the same time. As a preview, the processes are:

- **Input processing** (how learners make sense out of the language they hear and how they get "linguistic data" from it);
- System change, which involves two subprocesses: **accommodation** (how learners actually incorporate a grammatical form or structure into the "mental picture" of the language they are creating) and **restructuring** (how the incorporation of a form or structure can cause a ripple effect and make other things change without the learner ever knowing);
- **Output processing** (how learners acquire the ability to make use of the implicit knowledge they are acquiring to produce utterances in real time, e.g., during conversation).

These processes in turn have subprocesses, so that the learner's brain is manipulating various things at once. Unlike sitting down to study a set of instructions on how to install an overhead light, learning a language takes multitasking to the maximum degree.

Here is a simple test about common phenomena. Decide whether each statement is true or false.

- When babies learn how to walk, they just stand up and start walking.
- When learning a skill, it is not unusual for learners to plateau at some point (go through a period of not really improving), then begin to improve again. Sometimes they may even backslide a bit before they begin to improve again.

If you're like many people, you probably said "false" and "true" (or "probably true"). These answers reflect your unconscious understanding that learning is a dynamic process. For example, babies first have to learn how to stand up. They may wobble. They generally hold on to things for a while when "walking." When they start letting go, they often walk a few steps and then plop down. In short, learning to walk comes in stages. When attempting to improve backhand shots in tennis, a person may plateau for a while, hitting some backhand shots and getting them over the net but not with much power or spin. In learning to develop these other aspects of the shot, that person might miss more shots than usual as he or she attempts to alter body, wrist, or foot position. His or her ability with backhand shots seems to decline before it improves.

The same is true for SLA but on a much bigger scale. The implicit system that learners create evolves over time. It is never static; pieces and parts can be evolving while others are at rest. What does this evolution in the implicit system look like? In SLA, we have well-documented **developmental stages** for certain phenomena that suggest how this system evolves. In the acquisition of English as a second language, for example, it is well established that learners go through certain transitional stages on their way to native-like ability with negation:

1. The first stage is the simple placement of *no* in front of that which is to be negated: *No drink beer, No bike, No have car,* and so on.
2. The second stage involves the use of complete sentences, but the negator *no* is now placed internally rather than in front: *I no drink beer, He no has bike, We no have car.*
3. The third stage involves the incorporation of *don't* and sometimes *can't,* but as unanalyzed chunks of language that simply replace the *no* from the previous stage: *I don't drink beer, He don't/can't has bike,* and so on.
4. The final stage involves the acquisition of auxiliaries, fully analyzed *don't* (meaning the learners now have *do* as an functioning auxiliary), and the correct placement of *not*: *I don't (do not) drink beer, He doesn't have a bike.*

Some stages are what we call U-shaped because if we graph accuracy over time on an *x* and *y* axis, we get a U-shaped curve (Figure 1.1).

The learner starts out doing something correctly, dips down during acquisition, and then once again exhibits competence with the structure. One example involves past tense formation in English. First, learners correctly produce

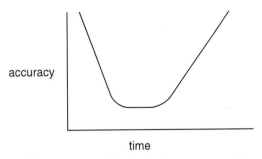

FIGURE 1.1 A U-shaped curve representing the uneven acquisition of certain language structures over time.

irregulars such as *went, came,* and *ate.* Then, as they begin to incorporate regulars (*watched, talked,* and so on), they begin to produce incorrect versions of the irregulars (*wented, goed, ated, eated*). Eventually these "regularized" irregulars are replaced by the forms the learners started out with. (We will see why this happens in Chapter 3.)

Developmental stages have been observed for many phenomena in SLA not only in English but also in German, French, Spanish, Swedish, and some other languages. These stages are seen to exist in both classroom and nonclassroom learners—remember, context does not affect these things—and in some cases, the stages look surprisingly like the same stages that children pass through when learning a first language. Stages are not neat, so we shouldn't think of some rigid move through stages like walking through different doors. A learner could be in stage 3 of acquiring a structure, have vestiges of stage 2, and also show signs of stage 4 emerging. This is one of the aspects of the learning process that makes SLA so dynamic.

Pause to consider . . .

what developmental stages might suggest about SLA. Does the following statement seem to be a logical conclusion to you? *All learners internalize language in the same way, no matter what. Why or why not?*

Other phenomena observed in SLA are called **acquisition orders.** Acquisition orders refer to the sequential acquisition of certain features of grammar (inflections, articles, copular or "linking" like *to be,* and others) over time. (*Sequential acquisition* refers to the fact that X precedes Y which in turn precedes Z during the course of learning.) In short, what learners demonstrate is that they gain mastery over grammatical forms in a predictable order, with mastery defined as a certain level of accuracy in their speech. These orders do not match instructional orders; that is, the order in which learners gain mastery does not necessarily match the order in which these things were taught in a classroom. In English, for example, learners always master the verbal inflection

–*ing* before regular past tense forms; and they always master past tense forms before present tense third-person –*s* (*he takes, she watches*). This order of mastery occurs with classroom learners as well, even though they may be taught the third-person rule before learning about past tense.

Acquisition orders have been explored in Spanish, German, and several other languages in addition to English. As in the case of stages, learners don't acquire one form first and then go on to acquire another. Usually, they are in the process of acquiring many forms and structures at once. A learner could gain mastery of one form and have partial mastery of others and literally no mastery of another. Again, this makes for a dynamic and constantly fluctuating system. (This picture is quite different from what many language textbooks would lead a person to believe.)

Some people confuse acquisition orders with developmental stages. One way to understand the difference is to remember that the term *acquisition orders* refers to the order in which different and independent pieces of language are mastered over time. The term *developmental stages* refers to the way in which one single aspect of language is acquired over time. So, plural –*s* might fall somewhere in the middle of the acquisition order of English inflections, but that tells us little about how plural –*s* is actually acquired. We could then look at the developmental stages in the acquisition of plural –*s*, which are phonological in nature. For example, a first stage would be not to mark plurals at all, as in *two dog*. A second might be to mark plurals but not use the full range of inflections; English has the sounds –s (*clocks*), –z (*dogs*), and –ez (*churches*) to make plurals. Subsequent stages would include the use of the other inflections or plural sounds.

Regardless of whether we examine developmental stages or acquisition orders, acquisition takes time. For learners of English, it often takes many years to gain mastery over the third-person –*s*. It takes learners of Spanish many years to gain control over the subjunctive mood, and it takes learners of French many years to gain control over the way in which the past tenses are used to communicate aspect (that is, the way in which we view an action in the past; e.g., was it in progress or not at a particular point in time?). It takes a number of years for learners to traverse developmental stages. Nothing about SLA as far as we can tell is either instantaneous or quick.

Pause to consider . . .

vocabulary learning. Do you think learning vocabulary is different from learning grammar in terms of time? That is, can vocabulary be acquired instantaneously? What is involved in learning a vocabulary item (that is, what must be learned)?

STATEMENT 4: MOST L2 LEARNERS FALL SHORT OF NATIVE-LIKE COMPETENCE

If you have or had grandparents from "the old country" or know people who do, you have probably noticed that their English is not native-like compared to that of someone born and raised in the United States. Their pronunciation may sound non-native, their syntax (sentence structure) may be non-native, their morphological system (inflections on words) may be non-native, and the way in which they use words may be non-native. Often everything about their language is non-native. Similarly, after years of learning high school and college French, someone might lament, "I can get by, but that's about it," suggesting that he or she falls far short of being native-like in that particular language. And many people who spend time abroad as part of a program in French, Japanese, Spanish, or German return to the United States much more competent and able in the language than they were when they left but still not native-like.

What all these scenarios point to is that in general, L2 learners do not become native-like in their abilities; some or all aspects of the system do not reach the target. For example, if we refer back to developmental stages and orders of acquisition, we see that some learners go through all or most of the stages and some do not. Some climb quite high in the acquisition orders while others reach mastery of only a few of the items. Why so many learners do not get through all stages or master all items represented by acquisition orders is not clear. Is it due to lack of instruction? No, because some people with little or no instruction acquire a great deal and some with a lot of instruction do not. So, ultimate attainment in the L2 cannot be due to instruction. Is the phenomenon due to age? Some have offered the **Critical Period Hypothesis,** which posits a critical period, a point beyond which the acquisition of a language is almost impossible. We address this matter in Chapter 5 and will simply say here that it is not clear there is such a thing as a critical period. And to be sure, some people are indistinguishable from natives in terms of what they can know and do.

The point we should understand is that *non-nativeness is natural and typical.* It is also natural and typical that people fall on a large *range of non-nativeness* and the level of non-nativeness may not be the same from one person to the next. As we mentioned earlier, some learners gain more control over developmental stages than others and some master more grammatical forms than others. What is more, one person might have very good control over syntax but have a heavily accented pronunciation. Another might have excellent control over both those areas. Another might not have very good control over either. Some research has shown that learners who are not native-like in their speech can make almost native-like judgments on sentences, reflecting an implicit system that has some native-like qualities. All these different learners could be speakers of the same first language who have undergone very similar if not identical L2 experiences.

It used to be that non-nativeness was taken to be a sign of failure, that somehow something went wrong or the learning experience didn't provide for the right kind of feedback. This is not the view any more, at least with scholars in SLA; non-nativeness is generally assumed to be the outcome in SLA. Yet there are examples in the literature of learners with clearly non-native grammar and pronunciation who are successful communicators and have led productive social and professional lives in the L2 environment. What SLA research has yet to determine is just why the phenomenon of non-nativeness exists and why people seem to exhibit such wide variation in their non-nativeness.

Pause to consider . . .

folk wisdom on this issue. Have you heard people say, "Children can pick up a second language easily"? What do they mean by easily? Do you agree with this statement? Some research shows that adolescents and adults have the advantage in the short run in that they can learn a lot of language and use a lot of language very early in the process of acquisition. Children, however, are better in the long run; they may not be as fast in the beginning, but they get further in the end. What do you think of this finding?

STATEMENT 5: SKILL ACQUISITION IS DIFFERENT FROM THE CREATION OF AN IMPLICIT SYSTEM

A look at a dictionary suggests something like the following for an everyday use of the term *skill: the ability to put some kind of knowledge to use accurately and easily.* Whether it be a sport, a craft, a medical procedure, or an academic essay, we might comment on someone's "skilled ability." We see that the person performs a task quickly or fairly effortlessly and may not need to stop and think about what he or she is doing at any given moment. In SLA, we can use the term similarly and talk about the acquisition of **skill** in the following way: the ability to use language accurately and without effort. In Chapter 4 we discuss the acquisition of skill and probe this definition a little more deeply; for now, we need to turn our attention to an important understanding about the difference between having an implicit system and having skills associated with it.

In the previous section, we mentioned in passing the person whose speech is not native-like yet who exhibits certain native-like intuitive or implicit knowledge about the way the language works. As one example, let's recall the *wanna* examples from the discussion of Statement 1 in this chapter. We noted earlier that for speakers of English, *Who do you wanna invite to the party?* is a perfectly fine sentence, whereas *Who do you wanna bring the potato chips to the party?* is not. I've used this example in graduate classes, and non-native speakers of English are in agreement with their native colleagues. However, when listening to my non-native students speak, I never hear the use of the contraction. They always say *want to.* This example illustrates the difference between having or developing an implicit system and having *productive use* of that system. *Wanna* is the result of rapid speech (English is full of these kinds of "reductions") and rapid speech is a result of skill development. The ability to know that *wanna* is good in one instance but not in another and yet to not use the contraction is only possible if the development of a system and the development of skill are two different things. My non-native students, then, have *wanna* in their implicit systems along with the rules that constrain its use, but they don't speak rapidly enough in English to actually produce the contraction.

Here is another example of the dissociation between an implicit system and a skill. A learner of a language must often learn to distinguish between sounds. In English, for example, *cook* and *kook* are different. The change in the vowel sound means the difference between someone working in a kitchen and someone who is missing some marbles. A native speaker of Italian (a friend I knew) would say such things as, "She's a very good kook," meaning she's very able in the kitchen. However, when we tested him on sound discrimination, he could hear the difference; that is, when asked which refers to someone in the kitchen—"He's a cook" or "He's a kook"—he always got such discriminations right. This suggests that somewhere in his system, he had the different vowel sounds mapped out, but he could not make productive use of them. Having an implicit system does not always mean that a person can use it expressively.

Very often in SLA research and in talking about SLA in general outside of the context of research and theory, we fail to make the distinction between the acquisition of a system and the acquisition of skill. What is more, we often take the skill aspect of SLA to be the hallmark of acquisition. When we say that someone is not proficient or competent in English, we usually mean that the person sounds definitively non-native. However, we cannot really make any comments about the underlying linguistic system and any discriminations that system might be able to make if we rely on how the person's speech sounds. We will see in Chapter 4, though, that learners' increasing fluency and accuracy over time, at least in terms of syntax and grammatical features, are largely dependent on the implicit system and what it contains.

Interestingly, language teachers are often fooled by what they think is their students' control over an L2 structure because the students can produce it. In research that my colleagues and I have conducted, we have seen learners' ability to use direct object pronouns in certain kinds of productive tasks in Spanish. In controlled tasks, they produce things such as *Juan la conoce* to express *John knows her*. Teachers applaud this and think, "Great." At the same time, when we give these learners sentences that involve object-verb-subject word order (which is not uncommon in Spanish), they misinterpret the sentence. They hear *La conoce Juan* (again, *Johns knows her* but said as *her knows John*) and think it means "She knows John"! Again, the fact that learners are able to produce something does not necessarily mean that they have an implicit system that actually has "etched in" a concept like object pronouns and how they are used in a language like Spanish. In this case, the pronoun itself may be etched in but the syntactic rule that governs its use is not. Learners may be using a certain kind of explicit knowledge to produce the sentence and may even develop some skill with that explicit knowledge, but the implicit system itself does not contain the rule. We discuss explicit knowledge further in later chapters.

Pause to consider . . .

that learners generally report that for some time they must "think in the first language" and then perform some kind of "mental translation" in order to make a sentence in the second language. Do you think that early- and intermediate-stage learners are tapping an implicit system to do this? If not, how are they able to make sentences in the L2 without some kind of elaborate if not fully functional underlying system?

FINAL COMMENTS

We saw in this chapter that the five statements about SLA are true regardless of context. What is interesting about context is that the statements hold even when learners receive instruction in the language and practice it as part of the classroom experience. Thus, stages exist whether you learn in a classroom or not. Acquisition orders exist whether you learn in a classroom or not. People do not reach L2 native-like competence whether they are in classrooms or not. People form implicit linguistic systems whether they are in classrooms or not, and so on. If you are wondering, "Does instruction then make no difference?" you are already ahead of the game. We address that question later in this book.

Pause to consider . . .

an assumption that underlies the five statements in this chapter: *language acquisition is different from any other kind of learning.* A belief that most theorists and researchers in SLA share is that learning a second language involves processes and parts of the brain that are different from those used to learn other things. Have you ever thought about the fact that when you learn just about anything (a recipe, history, how to tie your shoes, how to type), you learn it *through language*? Language is the medium by which you learn these things. It is a tool we use to acquire knowledge and skills, perhaps the most important tool we have as humans. Can you think of anything you don't normally learn through language? If language is unique to humans, is it possible that the brain has evolved in a way that treats language separately from other human cognitive abilities?

SUMMARY

In this chapter, we have reviewed five givens about SLA. We have seen that SLA involves the creation of an implicit system, that acquisition is slow yet dynamic, and that the entire process is complex and not reducible to one phenomenon. This latter point is particularly important since the next three chapters focus on the complexity of SLA and the various processes and knowledge sources involved in it. We also noted that non-native-like competence is the norm for L2 learners and that this is not deemed as a negative thing as it once was. Finally, we distinguished between the acquisition of competence and the acquisition of skill, a point that will be developed further in another chapter.

Implied in the discussion so far is that SLA is guided by **internal factors** that are difficult (if not impossible, in some cases) to affect from the outside. By internal factors we mean that the learner comes to the task of SLA equipped with linguistic mechanisms, predispositions regarding language, and certain processing constraints and strategies that interact to create the implicit linguistic system. In short, in spite of the fact that SLA happens in a social context (such as a classroom, a job, or a foreign country), the actual creation of a second language system happens in the mind or brain. It is the "stuff" that learners have in their minds that acts on the linguistic data to which they are exposed. In the next three chapters we explore what happens internally to the L2 learner during the course of acquisition.

READ MORE ABOUT IT

In this and all **Read More about It** sections, ▲ indicates that a reading may be particularly challenging for the beginning student of SLA.

A More Complete List of Givens

Long, M. H. (1990). The least a theory of second language acquisition must explain. *TESOL Quarterly, 24,* 649–666.

Also consult one of the more general books on SLA for givens in SLA research and theory.

Transitional Stages and Acquisition Orders

Bailey, N., Madden, C., & Krashen, S. D. (1974). Is there a natural sequence in adult second language learning? *Language Learning, 21,* 235–243.

Cazden, C., Cancino, E., Rosansky, E., & Schumann, J. (1975). *Second language acquisition in children, adolescents and adults.* Final report submitted to the National Institute of Education, Washington, D.C.

Dulay, H., & Burt, M. (1974). Natural sequences in child second language acquisition. *Language Learning, 24,* 37–53.

Hatch, E. M. (1978). *Second language acquisition: A book of readings.* Rowley, MA: Newbury House. [This book contains some of the readings listed here and more. Many of these are "foundation" readings in SLA.]

Larsen-Freeman, D., & Long, M. H. (1991). *An introduction to second language acquisition research.* New York: Longman. [See Chapter 4.] ▲

Raven, R. (1968). Language acquisition in a second language environment. *International Review of Applied Linguistics, 6,* 165–185.

Non-Nativeness

Bailystok, E., & Hakuta, K. (1994). *In other words.* New York: Basic Books. [See Chapter 3, Brain.]

Harley, B., & Wang, W. (1997). The Critical Period Hypothesis: Where are we now? In A. M. B. de Groot & J. F. Kroll (Eds.), *Tutorials in bilingualism: Psycholinguistic perspectives* (pp. 19–51). Mahwah, NJ: Erlbaum.

Johnson, J. S., & Newport, E. (1989). Critical period effects in second language learning: The influence of maturational state on the acquisition of English as a second language. *Cognitive Psychology, 21,* 60–99. ▲

Explicit and Implicit Systems and Learning

Ellis, N. (Ed.). (1994). *Implicit and explicit learning of languages*. London: Academic Press. ▲

Hulstijn, J., & Schmidt, R. (1994). Consciousness in second language learning. *AILA Review, 11.* [*AILA,* pronounced "eye-la," is the acronym for the Association Internationale de Linguistique Appliquèe.] ▲

Underwood, G. (1996). *Implicit cognition*. Oxford: Oxford University Press. [See especially the contributions by Berry and by Dienes & Perner.] ▲

VanPatten, B., & Mandell, R. (1999, March). *How type of structure influences the ways in which L2 learners render grammaticality judgments.* Paper delivered at the annual meeting of the American Association for Applied Linguistics, Stamford, CT.

CHAPTER 2

Input

Every scientific discipline has what can be called fundamental discoveries. These are discoveries that revolutionize the way in which the science continues to look at the phenomena under scrutiny. For astronomy, one such fundamental discovery was determining that the earth revolved around the sun. For biology, a fundamental discovery was that species evolve. In clinical psychology, one of the greatest fundamental discoveries was that there was something called the subconscious.

Although SLA as a scientific discipline is only four decades old, one of the most fundamental discoveries that revolutionized the way people thought about how languages are learned involved the concept of *input*. Although it might be a bit grandiose to imply that the discovery of the role of input is on par with the discovery of the earth's rotation or the existence of the subconscious, the point here is that in the small world of SLA research, the discovery of the role of input completely altered the way in which scholars conceptualized how languages are acquired. Today, all theories in SLA research accord input an important if not critical role in how learners create linguistic systems. In this chapter, we review the construct of input and what we know about how learners make use of it to create linguistic systems.

WHAT IS INPUT?

We've all heard people say something like, "I would really like your input on this." When they say this, they usually mean that they want advice, feedback, reflection, or some other such information that might help them make a decision or come to a conclusion regarding a problem or question they have. The word *input* used in this way refers to some kind of explicit information about something. This is the common, everyday use of the term.

In SLA, however, the word *input* has a very specific meaning. **Input** is the *language that a learner hears (or reads) that has some kind of communicative intent.* By *communicative intent* we mean that there is a message in the language that the learner is supposed to attend to; his or her job is to understand that message, to comprehend the meaning of the utterance or sentence. In first language acquisition, children are bombarded with input as caretakers talk to them all the time. "Are you hungry? Huh? Is that why you're crying? Are you hungry?" may be said to a six-month-old. This is input. "Where are you going? I don't want you touching that, okay?" might be said to a 14-month-old who has begun to toddle everywhere around the house. This, too, is input. These examples of language are input for acquisition because they exist within a communicative context; they are meaning-bearing utterances.

L2 learners get input as well. "You need to fill out this form. Here, see? Fill this out. Sign it here, on this line," might be said to an immigrant. This is input for that learner. "Open your books to page 24. Is everyone on page 24?" might be said in German to a first-semester German class in college. This is input to those learners. As in the case of L1 acquisition, these examples are considered input because they are couched within some kind of communicative context; somebody is speaking in the second language and attempting to communicate something. The job of the learner is to comprehend the message.

Thus, input is related to comprehension in that whenever a learner of a language is engaged in actively trying to comprehend something in the L2, that learner is getting input and that input serves as the basis for acquisition. The message the learner attempts to comprehend is encoded linguistically with lexical items (words), syntax (sentence structure), morphology (inflections on words), and so on. As a learner is grasping the meaning, he or she is making connections between meaning and how that meaning is encoded. Without an attempt at comprehension (a primary focus on getting meaning), there can be no connections between meaning and how it is encoded. For this reason we say that *acquisition happens as a by-product of comprehension.*

You can see, then, how this definition of *input* differs from the common, everyday use of the term. Input for acquisition is *not* information *about* the language. Learning a rule is not input. Input for acquisition is *not* drilling or filling out an exercise to practice verb forms. When learners produce language, they are not getting input. Language used for display purposes or for correction is not input. The term *display purposes* refers to instances in which teachers use language to model a rule and not to communicate. Thus, when an instructor corrects an ESL student who pronounces the *-ed* ending of the past tense as a full syllable by saying, "Not 'talkED.' Talk[t]. Talk[t]," this speech is not input for acquisition. Only instances of the L2 that are used to communicate information or to seek information can be considered as input for acquisition. (The conclusion here should not be that corrections are useless or telling learners about language is useless—we take that point up in Chapter 5. The point here is only that these instances do not represent the kind of primary input used for the creation of an implicit linguistic system.)

If you read more about SLA, you will find that other terms are used with the same meaning or to express a similar role for input: *primary linguistic data*, *the linguistic environment*, and *ambient speech*. Essentially these terms all attempt to capture the same two fundamental features:

- language directed to the learner or language that the learner hears in the speech around him or her; it is not language the learner produces;

- language with a communicative intent; the learner's communicative job is to capture the message or meaning contained in the utterance or sentence, that is, the learner's primary or focal attention is on meaning.

Another feature of input that is important for acquisition purposes is that it must somehow be *comprehensible*. If the learner's job is to grasp the message contained in what is said to him or her, then that message must be retrievable in some way from the input utterance. Language that is completely incomprehensible to the learner will not be of much use. Incomprehensible language can suddenly become comprehensible under certain circumstances (e.g., the learner grasps the meaning because of context or a visual clue and thinks, "Aha! That's what she's saying to me."), thus becoming input for acquisition.

There are, in essence, two major types of input: conversational and nonconversational. *Conversational input* is the language that learners hear in the context of some kind of communicative exchange with other people. It is language directed to the learners to which some kind of response is expected. The learner has to be part of the interaction for language to be conversational input; this is a critical part of our distinction, as we will soon see. Everyday conversations, classroom interactions in the L2, and playing games are all examples of situations in which learners can receive conversational input. *Nonconversational input* is language that a learner hears when he or she is not part of the interaction; it is not directed to the individual learner. Watching television, listening to the radio, and attending a formal lecture are all examples of getting nonconversational input. The language is not directed to the learner (in the case of the lecture, it is directed to the group), and the learner does not engage the other speaker in any kind of interaction. (Note: We have focused only on aural input and have ignored written input. The reason for this is that not all SLA contexts involve access to written texts or involve literate learners. In classroom contexts, written input may serve as linguistic input as well, but the connections between reading and the development of an implicit linguistic system have yet to be explored in any detail. And of course, with learning sign language, the input is not aural but visual.)

Pause to consider . . .

these two different kinds of input. Do you think there are any linguistic differences between conversational and nonconversational input? As you reflect on this, think about the following: level of formality, length of utterances, relative number of questions versus statements, incomplete sentences, range or type of vocabulary. You may come up with some other features on your own.

WHY IS INPUT IMPORTANT?

You may have heard of the tragic case of Genie, an adolescent who was rescued from an abusive family environment. For all of her developing years, Genie was locked away in a room by herself and isolated from nearly all contact with family and other humans. She thus received none of the warmth, love, or environmental stimuli that any child reared in a normal home would receive, nor did she ever hear language spoken.

Aside from the emotional and intellectual effects this isolation had on Genie, it was clear that it had a profound impact on her linguistic skills. When found, Genie basically had no first language. Reared almost as if she were a caged animal, Genie was deprived of the input needed for linguistic development. Raised in a situation in which there was no language directed to her, her brain had no opportunities to work on language as is normally the case. (And, as was suggested in Chapter 1, the consequences of language deprivation are devastating. Since we use language as an important tool for learning everything in life, without language it's not clear what Genie could learn or how her mind developed.)

The case of Genie points to the need for a child to be exposed to language in a natural environment if language acquisition is to happen. The conclusion in SLA research is much the same. Susan Gass, a noted scholar in SLA theory and research, puts it this way:

> The concept of input is perhaps the single most important concept of second language acquisition. It is trivial to point out that no individual can learn a second language without input of some sort. In fact, no model of second language acquisition does not avail itself of input in trying to explain how learners create second language grammars. (Gass, 1997, p.1)

Why do researchers concur on this point? Why do all theories in SLA use input in some way to explain acquisition? The argument—and evidence—basically boils down to the following: *Every successful learner of a second language has had substantial exposure to input as part of the process of language learning.* By *successful* we mean learners who have reached a fairly advanced stage of recognizable fluency and accuracy in use of the second language. This does not necessarily mean they are native-like, but they may be fairly close.

Additional evidence for the role of input comes from comparisons of **immersion** programs versus foreign language programs. Immersion programs are those in which learners learn content such as science, history, or psychology via the second language; the second language is the medium of instruction in these areas. Results of the research show that although their language is still not native-like, immersion learners are far superior to foreign language learners in terms of second language acquisition. Two differences are evident between the two contexts of learning: time on task (immersion involves more contact hours) and communicative input (immersion is nothing but communicative input).

One of the clearest examples of the critical role that input plays occurs in the study-abroad experience that many foreign language majors undergo. For example, a major in Spanish in a college in the Midwest might decide to go to Spain on a junior year abroad. In that situation, he or she might live with a host family, attend classes at the university taught entirely in Spanish, make friends with Spanish speakers, go to movies, watch TV, read the newspaper, and so on.

In short, the learner is surrounded by communicative language: input. The result for most people is a great leap in the development of both the implicit system and the skills that draw on that implicit system during language use.

To be sure, the fact that input is fundamental does not necessarily suggest that classroom learning of languages is not helpful. Nor does it suggest that feedback to learners is without merit. The conclusion that we have come to is that *instruction in language without input is basically senseless for acquisition.* It may be fine for learning about the language—and every student of formal linguistics learns a good many facts about languages such as Swahili, Tagalog, and Urdu while studying such things as phonology, morphology, and syntax. But this is *learning about language;* this is not *language learning.* The role of SLA instruction is to augment and help direct whatever internal processes learners bring to the task of learning language from the input they hear (and read).

Pause to consider . . .

the distinction just made: learning about language versus language learning. Had you made this distinction before? Although we consider language to be special and to involve certain language-specific mechanisms, what similar contrasts can you make in other domains?

HOW DO LEARNERS GET LINGUISTIC DATA FROM THE INPUT?

In this section we treat the topic of how learners get linguistic data while listening (or reading) in a second language. As previewed in Chapter 1, we call this *input processing.* Input processing consists of at least two subprocesses, each of which we discuss below: making form–meaning connections and parsing. Making **form–meaning connections** means getting such things from the input as that *–s* on the end of a verb in English means someone else or third person singular, that *–ato* in Italian refers to an event in the past, and that *chien* means dog in French. In other words, we are talking about connecting particular meanings to particular forms, be they grammatical forms or lexical (word) forms. **Parsing** refers to mapping syntactic structure onto the utterance, for example, knowing which noun is the subject and which is the object when hearing a sentence. We look at making form–meaning connections first.

Making Form–Meaning Connections

Below are four sentences in four different languages. If you know any of the languages, do not look at those sentences; cover them up with a pencil. See if you can understand the sentences in a language you don't know.

(1) German: Sylvia ist nicht nur intelligent, sondern auch fleissig.
(2) French: Sylvia n'est pas seulement intelligente mais aussi travailleure.

(3) Spanish: Sylvia no es sólo inteligente sino también trabajadora.

(4) Japanese: Silvia wa ataka ga il dake zya naku, yoku benkyoo simasu.

What were you able to comprehend? A little? A lot? Nothing? A number of factors come into play in how you comprehend the sentence. These factors include, among others, similarity between languages: Did you recognize any words? Was sentence structure a clue you used? But chances are better than 90 percent that the very first thing you did was look to see if you recognized any words. Why is this? Because as a speaker of one or more languages you already know that words exist and that words carry meaning. Unlike a child first language learner who has to discover that there are words and what they are and mean, you don't have to pass though that same first step in acquisition.

Now, without looking back, what do you remember about the following in the language that you do not know?

- verb form(s) used
- basic word order
- how negation is formed
- whether or not there is agreement between nouns and adjectives

Again, chances are better than 90 percent that you do not have any idea about most if not all of these aspects of the sentences. This test demonstrates one of the fundamental characteristics of input processing in an L2: When listening with intent to comprehend, learners apply whatever strategies they can to get meaning. One of the first strategies is *to seek out content words,* because L2 learners know the difference between **content words** (the "big" words) and non-content words (the "little" words). We can translate this into a principle for input processing and its first corollary:

P1. Learners process input for meaning before anything else.

P1a. Learners process content words before anything else.

What this means is that when attempting to get at the meaning of input, if you are struggling with basic comprehension, you will most likely *not* process any formal features of language. Every person possesses what is called **working memory**. Working memory is that "space" in your head where you conduct second-by-second if not millisecond-by-millisecond processing of information. As you process language during comprehension, you briefly hold bits and parts of it in your working memory.

If you're old enough or watch Nick at Nite (a television show in the United States), you may have seen the episode of "I Love Lucy" in which Lucy and Ethel get jobs working in a chocolate factory. Their job is to wrap chocolates coming down a conveyor belt. At the beginning, when the conveyor belt is going slowly, the job is easy. But when their supervisor sees that they can handle more, she yells "Speed it up." The belt begins to move faster and faster. Soon, the belt is delivering chocolates at a pace beyond Lucy's and Ethel's capacity to wrap them. To keep from getting fired, they end up stuffing chocolates in their dresses, hats, and pockets to hide them from their supervisor.

Working memory resembles Lucy's and Ethel's efforts. If capacity is not exceeded (task demands aren't too great), you're fine. But if task demands exceed what you can do, processing deteriorates. Your working memory simply does not have enough capacity to do much more than search for content words—and even then you might not get them all at the beginning stages of learning. What you actually hold and process in working memory is called **intake**. At first, intake consists of content words only (or mostly).

Words can also mean whole chunks of language that the learner cannot "analyze." Learners might hear things such as, "Where's the . . . ?" so many times that they actually create early on a chunk of language, "Wheresthe," with no internal parts to it; that is, they do not know that it actually consists of three words, one of which is contracted. For them, it is a chunk of language used to ask the location of something. In my own French, I have *Est-ce que . . .* as a chunk of language for asking questions. It got into my system without my analyzing it (until much later); I simply knew it was the way you asked a yes-or-no question. These types of chunks are called **prefabricated patterns**.

In other instances, learners store whole sentences they hear as big chunks. For example, a learner might hear and store as one whole unit "Idunno" and not know that it is a reduced form of "I do not know." In French, a learner might store *S'il vous plaît* as a chunk and not know it is a phrase that actually means "If it pleases you." These whole sentence chunks are called **routines**. Learners extract them from the input as large words and store them as large words. They do not know what the individual parts of each are. It is posited that even in native-language learning, we store prefabricated patterns and routines that never go away in life. These are part of our "mental lexicon" (vocabulary) much as "cat," "steal," and "happy" are. Many of these patterns are common, everyday social routines such as "How do you do?" which is uttered in certain contexts and is probably not generated word by word but as a single large chunk.

How do learners attend to form? Let's look at another example. Keep this sentence in mind but don't refer back to it: "Yesterday Sylvia walked to the university with her friend Jane the Crazed." Now, select a sentence from a language you don't know and read it. Don't dwell on it too much!

(5) Spanish: Ayer Sylvia caminó a la universidad con su amiga Juana la Loca.
(6) French: Hier Sylvie est marché à l'université avec son amie Jeanne la Folle.
(7) German: Gestern ging Silvia mit ihrer Freundin Jane, der Verrückten, zur Universität.
(8) Japanese: Kinoo Silvia wa ano tyotto henna tomodati Jane to daigaku made aruite ikimasita.

Cover the sentences up and answer this question: What's the past tense form equivalent to "walked" in the sentence you read? If you're highly attentive right now because of the topic we're working on, you might have noticed it. But, again, there is a 90 percent chance that under normal circumstances you would not have noticed the past tense form. However, if anyone asked you, "Is the action in the present, past, or future?" you could answer because you would have processed the equivalent of "yesterday." This word contains pastness in its meaning the same way the verb form does. One of the consequences of paying attention to content words, then, is that you can skip over a grammatical form if it carries the same meaning, that is, if there is **redundancy**. This process can be formalized as a second corollary to the first principle:

> P1b. Learners process content words before grammatical forms if they carry the same semantic information.

Here, of course, the phrase *semantic information* refers to meaning. Most grammatical forms carry meaning of some kind. They may indicate "when" or "who"; they may indicate a speaker's perspective ("I take this as a fact/I don't take this as a fact"); they may indicate social deference (formal vs. informal); or they may carry many other real-world meanings. But most grammatical forms are also redundant (although the redundancy varies with languages); the meaning these forms convey may be expressed elsewhere by words or phrases. Verb endings that indicate person number are almost always redundant in English and French because these languages generally require subject nouns or pronouns. These content words already carry the meaning of "who" or "which person." Spanish and Italian, on the other hand, allow omission of pronouns, so that you can say *Parlo italiano* (I speak Italian); only in certain discourse situations do you have to say *Io parlo italiano.* The bare verb *parlo* contains two pieces of information that in English and French, for example, require two words: *I speak, Je parle.*

Pause to consider . . .

whether there are grammatical forms that are never redundant or (almost) always redundant. Consider the following examples: (1) The suffix *–ing* in English refers to "action in progress." In a typical English construction that uses this form, is there a content word or even a phrase that means the same thing? (2) Regarding adjective agreement in the Romance languages (languages derived from Latin, such as Spanish and French), is gender expressed somewhere in a content word and not just on adjective endings?

Because learners are still processing only content words, *grammatical forms that are redundant do not contribute any real meaning to the sentence* in that the learner can skip over them. In this case, the learner's intake (the language processed and held in working memory) still basically consists of content words. Learners may attend to grammatical form if it carries meaning and is not redundant. Remember that the learner's purpose is to get meaning from the utterance. Nonredundant grammatical forms are more important for comprehension than redundant forms because they may be the sole bearer of a particular meaning in an utterance. When I hear in English, "What are you doing?" I rely on the *–ing* to let me know that the person is asking about any activity that is in progress as opposed to an activity recently completed or one that hasn't started yet or that I'm just about to start. We can capture this aspect of input processing in the following final corollary to the first principle.

> P1c. Learners tend to process more meaningful grammatical forms before grammatical forms of little or no meaning.

We might now envision the learner's intake consisting not only of content words but also perhaps of some grammatical forms, those that he or she had to process to get the meaning of the utterance.

Pause to consider . . .

redundancy one more time. Is a formal feature of language either redundant or not? Are there cases in which a form might be redundant in one sentence or utterance but be the sole provider of a particular meaning in another sentence and therefore not redundant? Hint: Compare in English the person-number *–s* in present tense with the past tense marker *–ed* in terms of the contexts in which they normally appear.

Let's think about a form that is always redundant or carries no meaning because it is semantically empty to begin with. Gender inflections on adjectives in Romance languages are good examples since they are both redundant and semantically empty (that is, they carry no meaning—*semantics* refers to meaning.) In a phrase like *la casa blanca* (the white house), the *–a* of *blanca* is redundant (the definite article is already marked the same way) and it carries no meaning, that is, "What does *–a* refer to in the real world?" If you answer, "Well, it means feminine. It shows gender," you are confusing biological gender with grammatical gender. Yes, in the real world there are men and women, stallions and mares, roosters and hens, bulls and cows, and so on; but a table is a table, a chair is a chair, a painting is a painting, and so on. With inanimate objects there are not two: one male and one female. So when adjectives agree in Italian, French, Spanish, and other languages, they are not reflecting any biological difference out there in the real world. The agreement is semantically empty. (It is rather unfortunate that linguists chose the term *gender* to describe the alternations such as *la table* and *le livre* in a language like French.) The question with these kinds of grammatical forms, then, is why would the learner ever pay attention to them? How does processing of these kinds of grammatical features in the input ever happen?

You will remember that we started out earlier saying that processing happens in working memory in a millisecond-by-millisecond fashion. Learners process only what they can for meaning, because their early-stage mechanisms cannot efficiently process everything. For the nonmeaningful types of grammatical forms to get processed, something has to happen so that working memory can release *attention* and *effort* to those items. What has to happen is that the meaning of the utterance must be comprehended without exhausting the *limited processing capacity of working memory*. Remember the test you took early in this chapter in which you read a sentence in a language you didn't know to see what you could glean from it? You focused on words. Here are the sentences again. This time, read them as many times as you want with the English gloss provided first: "Sylvia is not only intelligent, but also industrious (hardworking)."

(1) German: Sylvia ist nicht nur intelligent, sondern auch fleissig.
(2) French: Sylvia n'est pas seulement intelligente mais aussi travailleure.

(3) Spanish: Sylvia no es sólo inteligente sino también trabajadora.

(4) Japanese: Silvia wa ataka ga il dake zya naku, yoku benkyoo simasu.

Now that you know the meaning of the sentence, you are probably picking up things you missed before. You don't have to struggle to get the meaning and this frees up attention and effort to process things you would otherwise skip over. We can couch this in another principle for input processing:

> P2. For learners to process form of little or no meaning, they must be able to process the content or propositional message of an utterance with little or no cost to attentional resources.

Later in this chapter, we discuss some ways in which attention is freed up for learners, allowing them to attend to things they would miss otherwise.

Another important point for processing grammatical features in the input is **acoustic salience**. This aspect of language refers to the relative degree to which something "sticks out from the crowd" in an utterance. One factor that affects acoustic salience is stress, the relative loudness of pronunciation of a vowel. Something that carries strong stress is more salient than something that does not. If you listen to most languages, you will note that content words carry almost all the major stress points of the sentence. If someone said the following sentence to you in normal conversational English, the underlined items would carry stronger stress than those that are not underlined.

Mary <u>runs</u> as <u>fast</u> as <u>John</u> and can <u>generally</u> <u>beat</u> him in a <u>race</u>.

But since so many grammatical features in all kinds of languages do not carry stress, what may be more important for salience is where they appear in an utterance. There are three possibilities: at the beginning, at the end, and somewhere in between. What research has shown is that the *initial position* of an utterance is the most salient, the *final position* of the utterance is the next most salient, and the *middle parts of utterances* are the least salient. You can prove this by performing the following experiment. Record five sentences in another language that are about ten to twelve syllables long. The recording should be in normal conversational style. Then find people who do not speak that language. Have them listen to each sentence one at a time and then repeat the sentence as best they can. If you sample enough people, you will discover that the first parts of the utterances are repeated more than the ends of the utterances, which in turn are repeated more often than what's in the middle. Another principle for input processing, then, is this one:

> P3. Learners tend to process the beginnings of sentences best, followed by the ends of sentences. The middle of a sentence is the most difficult place to process grammatical form.

What this all means is that grammatical forms that are attached to words in initial position or themselves occur in initial position will be processed before forms in other positions (if we hold everything else constant!).

Input processing can be schematized as shown in Figure 2.1. The arrow leading from input to intake represents input processing, which is affected by the principles that guide how learners make form–meaning connections.

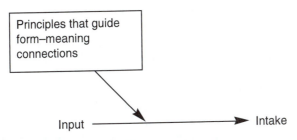

FIGURE 2.1 A preliminary sketch of input processing

> ## *Pause to consider . . .*
>
> where features like the following occur in utterances in the language you teach or will teach: past tense markers, subjunctive markers (if you have them in your language), articles, clause markers.

Parsing

The following sentence is incomplete. In how many distinct ways can you complete it to make a sentence of four to five words?

I have . . .

Depending on how you interpret the verb *have,* you basically have only two choices. You can complete the sentence with a noun or noun phrase: *I have a big house. I have three cats. I have loving children.* You can also complete it with a verb phrase: *I have already eaten. I have bought something. I have scored well.* This exercise demonstrates what must happen when you process a sentence during comprehension. When you encounter the verb *have,* you must make a determination about what kind of verb it is (auxiliary vs. "full" verb). The millisecond you do, your mind computes what must come next, a noun phrase or a verb phrase. You are literally projecting the syntax (structure) of the sentence at that moment and are hoping your expectations are fulfilled. This is what parsing is: *the projection of some kind of syntactic structure onto an utterance as we hear it.*

Parsing may also refer to filling in gaps. When you read or hear *John flew to Miami and Mary to Chicago,* you know that Mary flew as well. She didn't drive, ride a bike, or hop a train. What is missing after Mary is the verb *flew;* English doesn't require this verb in this particular position and can optionally delete it, but your parser is not confused. As it computes a syntactic structure for this particular sentence, it puts in a verb slot because all full sentences must have verbs. What your parser does is compute a sentence like *John flew to Miami and Mary [flew-DELETED] to Chicago.* (The gap, by the way, is called an *empty category.* Language is full of empty categories, but you have few problems in comprehending sentences because parsers are built to handle them.)

One of the fundamental aspects of parsing is figuring out who did what to whom. In English we rely on word order. *The man killed the lion* is a different sentence from *The lion killed the man*. As an English speaker, when you begin to parse the first sentence, you assign a noun phrase structure—that is, a noun and all the stuff that goes with it such as articles, adjectives, demonstratives, and so on—to *the man* and initially project that it will be a subject. When you hear the verb you project a verb phrase—the verb and all the stuff that goes with it—and because the particular verb is *kill* you expect there to be an object of the verb. Your expectations are confirmed as you hear *the lion*; the meaning you attach to the sentence is that the lion was killed by the man.

In some languages, however, word order is not the only clue to who did what to whom, and in some cases it isn't a clue at all. Some languages mark nouns for case (subject vs. object, for instance) clearly indicating for you (the listener) who did what to whom. In most such languages, word order then is not rigid as in English. Here are examples from Hungarian and Spanish. Note that Hungarian marks the object of the verb with an ending; Spanish marks the object with a preposition in front of the noun. (Kutya/perro = dog; maska/gato = cat; kergeti/caza = chases; the sentence means *The dog chases the cat*.)

(9a) A kutya kergeti a maska-t.
(9b) A maska-t kergeti a kutya.
(10a) El perro caza al gato.
(10b) Al gato lo caza el perro.

As you can see, both languages admit more than one word order to express the same concept. Native speakers, of course, have no difficulty in interpreting these sentences correctly. But what about L2 learners? Research has demonstrated that L2 learners tend to interpret all sentences as subject-verb-object, so they would misinterpret sentences 9b and 10b as *The cat chases the dog*. In short, *they parse the sentences incorrectly and project the wrong syntactic structure onto the sentence*. We can capture this in another principle:

P4. L2 Learners tend to interpret the first noun or noun phrase in an utterance as the subject of the sentence. This is called the first-noun strategy.

In L2 languages like English, this might work most of the time. One exception is passive constructions. How would L2 learners interpret the following?

The horse was kicked by the cow.

You're correct if you said that they would (tend to) misinterpret it as *The horse kicked the cow*. (Some research shows that this misinterpretation occurs even when two languages have the exact same passive construction, such as English and French. So, the problem is not an L1 vs. L2 problem.) The consequences of the first-noun strategy are, among other things, the following:

- delayed acquisition of case marking,
- delayed acquisition of pronouns in languages like Spanish and Italian that do not require subjects, and
- delayed acquisition of structures that don't follow the expected word order (e.g., passives, and verbs in Spanish and Italian like *gustar* and *piacere*, which mean "to please").

The delayed acquisition of case marking seems clear; why pay attention to case marking if you're using word order to comprehend instead? The learner simply skips over these. The delayed acquisition of pronouns in languages like Spanish and Italian may be subtler. In Spanish (and Italian), for example, object-verb-subject structures are possible, as illustrated in sentence 10b. But often, the first noun is not a noun but a pronoun. Here are some examples.

(11) *Nos faltan varios libros.* (We are missing several books.)
(12) *Me vio Marìa.* (Mary saw me.)
(13) *Se levanta.* (He/She gets up.)

In (11), the pronoun *nos* does not mean *we* but *to us*; the sentence literally means *To us several books are lacking* (*Several books are lacking to us*). In (12) *me* is not a subject; the sentence literally says *Me saw Mary* (*Mary saw me*). In (13) *se* does not mean *he* or *she* but is the reflexive pronoun that shows that the person (encoded in the verb form and nowhere else) is getting himself or herself up rather than someone else. In English it would be something like *Himself he gets up*. If learners process these sentences incorrectly, then the following is the result: *nos* = we, *me* = I, and *se* = he/she (depending on context). These forms compete with the actual subject pronouns, *nosotros*, *yo*, and *él/ella*, respectively. The result is a confused pronoun system and delayed acquisition of object and reflexive pronouns.

Pause to consider . . .

the effect of the first-noun strategy on picking up verb forms. In languages in which subjects are almost always present, such as English and French, why would a learner need to attend to verb forms? Since pronouns are content words in that they tell "who," wouldn't learners pay attention to those and ignore verb endings?

The first-noun strategy can be overridden by two processes: *lexical semantics* and *event probabilities*. **Lexical semantics** refers to what is required of an entity to perform the action expressed by the verb. Literally, lexical semantics involves the meaning of any word and the consequences of that particular meaning for sentence structure. For example, the lexical semantics of *bite* require that a subject noun represent the following characteristics: It must be animate, it must have a mouth, it must have teeth. On the other hand, the lexical semantics of *seem* do not require animacy, and therefore any other traits associated with animate beings are not necessary. Compare, for example, *John seems tired* and *That painting seems to be from the Renaissance period*. Going back to *bite*, which does require particular characteristics for its subject, if you heard a sentence in another language that did not conform to expected word order, such as *carrot-bite-horse*, you would probably not rely on the first-noun strategy since the verb does not allow something like *carrot* to be the subject; lexical semantics intervene to push you toward the correct interpretation.

Event probabilities refer to expectations in the real world. In this case, a verb may not rule out a particular noun being a subject, but our expectation of what normally happens in real life does. Once again, going back to *bite*, imagine you heard *man-bite-dog* in a language with flexible word order. Both *man* and *dog* possess the characteristics required by *bite*. You could conceivably think the man is biting the dog, but your normal interpretation would be to think the sentence must mean that the dog is biting the man. In other words, the event probability of who would bite whom would lead you to the correct interpretation.

We can revise Figure 2.1 to incorporate parsing. Now we see that at least two sets of processes are occurring at the same time during input processing, as captured in Figure 2.2.

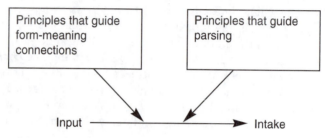

FIGURE 2.2 A revised sketch of input processing

DOES ANYTHING FACILITATE HOW LEARNERS PROCESS INPUT?

Have you ever been bombarded with so much information at once that when you walked away you could remember only one or two things? In such cases our working memory for processing information becomes taxed to the point of overload and little gets processed. You will remember that this is similar to what we said about getting grammatical form from input; the learner's working memory is even more taxed than a native speaker's, so that the acquisition of many formal features of language doesn't happen unless the comprehension of meaning comes easily (see P2). As learners become more and more proficient at listening comprehension in general, attention is freed up to get information from the input that was missed before. But processing form in the input is facilitated at all levels of learning if comprehension is somehow facilitated. How?

One way in which comprehension is facilitated is by **interaction**—that is, by conversation. During interactions, there may be *negotiation of meaning* as a speaker attempts to confirm what he or she just heard, attempts to verify that the other person is following, and so on. In face-to-face interactions that include negotiation of meaning, learners get to help "manage" what they hear, and sentences are often modified in such a way that something they missed before pops out at them. One way meaning is negotiated is through **confirmation checks,** which recast what the learner says. The following interchange took place in a tennis locker room. Bob is a native speaker of English and Tom is a lower-level non-native speaker with Chinese as a first language.

helping
process
input
—————
Interact

BOB: So where's Dave?
TOM: He vacation.
BOB: He's on vacation?
TOM: Yeah. On vacation.
BOB: Lucky guy.

Note how Tom corrects what he said the first time in response to Bob's question: *He vacation* ⟶ *[He] On vacation*. Although not completely correct, his second statement shows that he noticed a preposition in Bob's utterance. Why did this happen? Bob was not providing new information but simply recasting what Tom had said to confirm what he heard, so Tom did not need to process for meaning as much; the topic hadn't changed, and in fact the information was exactly the same. Tom's processing sources were freed up at that point, and he picked up on the preposition. The interaction, and specifically the confirmation check, which provided no new information but served a communicative intent ("Am I hearing you correctly?"), made the one sentence very comprehensible.

Another way in which attention can be freed up is by **modification** of input. This process works primarily when listening and reading materials are directly targeted toward learners. For example, TV is incomprehensible to most early-stage or lower-level learners and presents a challenge for most intermediate and some advanced-level learners. Learners struggle so much to get even the gist of what is being said that they have no attentional resources left over to process any form. Even watching something over and over again may not help. But when there is **simplification** of input, the comprehension burden can be eased. Have you ever seen how people talk to babies and to pets? Their language is very different from adult-to-adult language. Babies get good simplified input (at least in most cultures) that helps them "bootstrap" their way into comprehension and by extension into acquisition. (Too bad pets can't learn language!)

Input can be simplified in a number of ways, among which are using shorter sentences (less information to hold in working memory at any given time), adding pauses (breaks information up into shorter bits), using more common or known vocabulary (less to hold in working memory as learners search their mental lexicons for meaning), repeating something (allowing learners a second shot at meaning), and others. As we have seen, input is modified and simplified almost naturally in conversation. We tend to target our level of interactions with certain non-native speakers because we perceive them to be at a different level of language ability. My mother worked for a number of years in a bakery owned by an immigrant from Vietnam. Many of the customers were Vietnamese and had limited English abilities. I observed my mother a number of times as she waited on them, and I compared how she spoke to them with how she spoke to native English speakers. With English speakers the interactions would flow effortlessly. With the lower-level non-natives she would say things like, "Which ones you want? You want this one? (pointing) You want that one? How many? How many you want? Two? Three?" using short sentences, repetition, and the like. Instructors who use a lot of the L2 in the classroom simplify their speech in similar ways. (Note, however, that my mother, like many natives when talking to low-proficient non-natives, produced utterances that are actually ungrammatical in English: *How many you want?* vs. *How many do you want?* This kind of ungrammatical language forms part of the

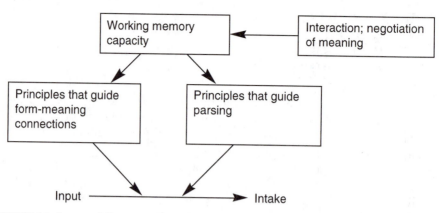

FIGURE 2.3 A more fully revised sketch of input processing

simplification of input known as **foreigner talk;** research has shown that this kind of talk emerges from natives when there is a perception of low proficiency and difference in social status. In classrooms, instructors engage in **teacher talk,** which often resembles foreign talk minus the ungrammaticality.)

The point here is that L2 learners don't need to get better at comprehending before they can *begin* to attend to grammatical features in the input. When the *input is adjusted for level,* learners have less of a comprehension burden and thus *the likelihood of their attending to form increases* (but it is not guaranteed!).

What we have just described—the role of interaction as an aid to working memory—can be penciled into our previous figure. The result is Figure 2.3, in which interaction doesn't affect the principles of input processing per se but rather has an impact on working memory, which influences how the principles play out.

Adjusting Input to level [handwritten note in margin]

Pause to consider. . .

the Bob and Tom dialogue. Do you think that Tom's noticing of the preposition and his subsequent use of it in his own speech meant that he had acquired it? Had the use of *on* as a preposition entered his developing system, his underlying mental representation of the language? Why or why not? (We will address this issue in Chapter 3.)

SUMMARY

In this chapter we examined the nature of input, defining it as language that learners hear or read and that they process for its informational content (message). We discussed the importance of the role of input in SLA and underscored that all successful learners have access to input and interaction with other speakers of the L2. We also reviewed in some detail the nature of input processing, that is, how learners make form–meaning connections and how they parse sentences.

- Learners always process input for meaning first and rely on content words before anything else to get that meaning.
- When a content word and a grammatical form encode the same meaning (e.g., pastness is encoded both by a time reference such as "yesterday" and a verb inflection such as –*ed*), learners rely on the content word and "skip" the grammatical form.
- Position in an utterance is important. Utterance initial position is the most salient; learners process elements that appear at the beginning of sentences before they process elements at the end or in the middle.
- Learners rely on a first-noun strategy to understand "who did what to whom."

A logical question after this discussion on input and input processing is this: What happens to the input after it gets processed? Does successful processing suggest that the learner has acquired a particular grammatical feature or structure? Answers to these questions form the basis of Chapter 3.

READ MORE ABOUT IT

The Importance of Input

Krashen, S. D. (1985). *The input hypothesis: issues and implications*. New York: Longman.

Input and Interaction

Gass, S. M. (1997). *Input and interaction and the second language learner*. Mahwah, NJ: Erlbaum.

Input Processing

Klein, E. (1999). Just parsing through: Notes on the state of L2 processing research today. In E. Klein & G. Martohardjono (Eds.), *The development of second language grammars: A generative approach* (pp. 197–216). Philadelphia: Benjamins.

VanPatten, B. (1996). *Input processing and grammar instruction*. Norwood, NJ: Ablex. ▲

VanPatten, B. (2000). Thirty years of input (or Intake: The neglected sibling). In B. Swierzbin, F. Morris, M. E. Anderson, C. A. Klee, and E. Tarone (Eds.), *Social and cognitive factors in second language acquisition* (pp. 287–322). Somerville, MA: Cascadilla.

Simplified Input

Hatch, E. (1983). Simplified input and second language acquisition. In R. W. Andersen (Ed.), *Pidginization and creolization as language acquisition* (pp. 64–86). Rowley, MA: Newbury House.

See also Gass (1997) under Input and Interaction for information on simplified and modified input during interactions.

CHAPTER 3

The Developing System

In Chapter 1, we saw that SLA involves the creation of an implicit or unconscious linguistic system. You also took some simple tests (judging sentences) to illustrate what we mean by *implicit*, namely, that this linguistic system exists outside of your consciousness; although you can use it and you "know" it's there, you really don't know how it got there or what rules govern it. You might *think* you know how it got there, but as we have seen, there is more to language acquisition than meets the eye.

In this chapter, we go into a bit more detail about the **developing system** and what it is (and isn't). We also look at some of the hidden processes that affect language learners without their knowing it. We say these processes are hidden because they operate involuntarily; the learner has no control over them. In fact, we might even say that the learner *experiences these processes* (unconsciously, of course) or better yet, that *these processes happen to the learner*. In the end, we compare this system with explicit knowledge, the system that the learner is aware of and worked purposely to obtain through conscious study or practice. Usually the learner is able to articulate a rule in some way or remembers part of what he or she learned (e.g., "In the past I learned that some French verbs take *avoir* and some take *etre*. I think it's motion verbs or something like that that take *etre*."). Before continuing, you might wish to review the discussion of the first "given" in Chapter 1—that SLA involves the creation of an implicit (unconscious) linguistic system.

WHAT IS THE DEVELOPING SYSTEM?

The term *developing system* contains two words. Stop and think for a moment about each and try to define them by completing each sentence that follows:

> The term *developing* refers to _____.
> A *system* is a _____.

The word *developing,* of course, refers to something that is in progress, evolving, changing, and perhaps not standing still. This is certainly characteristic of the L2 system as we saw in Chapter 1 in our discussion of the dynamic nature of that system. Your own L1 is also developing to a certain extent. How? Well, it's doubtful that you are learning much syntax at this point in your life; according to most models of child language acquisition, an L1 syntactic system is pretty much in place by the time a child begins elementary school. The same is true for the morphological and phonological components. (Recall that morphology refers to inflections on words as well as prefixes and suffixes and phonology refers to the sound system.) What do you think are the parts of your system that may still be subject to change or evolution? (Keep this question in mind, because after our discussion in this section of the chapter, you will be asked again!)

If you look up the word *system* in a dictionary, you might find something like the following: *A system is a complex unity consisting of many parts, often diverse in nature, that all work according to a shared or common purpose, plan, or goal.* If we break this sentence down we see several key ideas: *complex, unity, diverse, common purpose.* Systems are complex and thus not easy to describe. Compare the following. How would you describe each?

- an atom
- an airline company

If you remembered anything from basic physics and chemistry, you probably realized right away that it is much easier to describe an atom than an airline company. An atom consists of particles (e.g., neutrons, protons, electrons, and subparticles) held together by some kind of invisible force. But an airline company consists of dozens of components that interact in different ways, some directly with each other, some only indirectly, and some not at all, even though all are necessary for the airline company to function. A linguistic system is like an airline company in that it, too, is complex and not so easy to describe (but it is describable!).

Unity, of course, refers to different components forming a whole, working together. In the airline company, there are pilots, flight attendants, mechanics, ground crew, ticket agents, baggage handlers, airplanes, machinery, and many more components that all work together. A linguistic system also has multiple components that act as a whole. Each time you utter a sentence, or even a word, those components come together so that that sentence can be spoken.

In this day and age we are sensitive to the word *diversity.* We hear of diversity training, diversity issues, and so on. *Diverse* simply means different. In the airline company example, it is clear that pilots are not flight attendants nor are flight attendants the same as baggage handlers. Each has a different job, a different function to perform, and each group contributes uniquely to what an airline company finally is. A linguistic system is also composed of diverse components, many of which we discussed in Chapter 1. In this chapter, we revisit them a bit differently.

The last term, *common purpose,* is easy to grasp. For the airline company, the common purpose of all the diverse components is to provide a service to passengers. Each component has a specific job to do, but without that common purpose there would be no job to begin with. What is the common purpose of the components of a linguistic system? Look at the following list and decide which you believe is the common purpose.

- comprehension
- speech production
- learning
- social interaction

Did you answer that the linguistic system's purpose is all of the choices? Unique to human beings, the linguistic system indeed serves a variety of purposes that ultimately can be grouped under the rubric **communication**. A typical definition of *communication* in language circles is *the expression, interpretation, and negotiation of meaning in a given context.* It is easy to see that *comprehension* falls under this definition (it is similar to interpretation), and it is also easy to see that *speech production* falls under this definition (it is one type of expression—don't forget that sign languages are also human language systems, and people also write). If you think about *learning,* you see that it tends to happen through communication. You are reading at this moment and learning something about SLA by interpreting information from this book. That is communication. When you sit in a class and listen to a lecture or ask questions to clarify a point or relate one idea to another, that is communication. Every day of your life, you rely on communication to learn something. And communication is (partially) dependent on a linguistic system. (Language and communication, however, are not the same thing. Bees can communicate, as can dogs, but no one would say they have anything approaching a language or linguistic system as defined here. Have you ever heard of a dog performing a grammaticality judgment task?)

Social interaction is also partly dependent on a linguistic system. Have you ever gone down a hallway and had someone walk by and ignore you? You might turn to a coworker and say, "I wonder what's up with Jim? He walked right by and didn't *say* anything." You were expecting some kind of use of language as part of routine social interaction (e.g., you may have expected Jim to say, "Hi, how's it going?"). If you've ever been to a cocktail party and didn't know anyone, you may have struck up a conversation by saying something like, "Hi, my name is Nancy. How do you know John (the host)?" You are using communication in this instance to establish a relationship (no matter how superficial or profound). Establishing relationships relies in part on communication.

The point here, of course, is that communication and thus language permeate the lives of every normal functioning human being. Imagine what our culture(s) would be like without language! The task of an L2 learner is often to acquire enough language so that he or she can effectively communicate with others. Let's turn our attention now to the issue at hand: What makes up the developing system?

The language learner's developing system consists of a variety of linguistic components that interact in complex ways. In Chapter 1 we listed these components: the lexicon (words), phonology (the sound system), morphology (how words are formed), syntax (rules that govern sentence structure), and so on. In this chapter we are going to talk about the system as having three fundamental components: a network of associations, a syntactic component consisting of rules, and a set of competencies related to language use. Let's begin with the network.

Pause to consider . . .

the example of the airline company. Can any component of the airline company be deleted without affecting the company's ability to achieve its purpose? Review the components of a linguistic system in Chapter 1. Do you think the purpose of the system could still be served if any of those components were deleted?

The Network of Forms and Lexical Items

Have you ever thought about the World Wide Web? It is composed of thousands of servers and perhaps millions of sites that are linked by lines (optic fibers or some other tangible lines). A visual representation of the system would look something like the flight-route maps in the back of airline magazines, except the routes would be multiplied by thousands. Quite a network!

Current thinking about a person's implicit linguistic system also speaks to a complex and vast **network of forms and lexical items** in the brain. Let's take a simple example. The word *interest* would be connected to other words that contain the root form *interest* and that are related in meaning: *disinterest, interesting, uninteresting*. These in turn are connected to each other (Figure 3.1). Some of the items may be linked to others for semantic reasons, even though the words are not of the same root (Figure 3.2). But note that lexical items also have form. They may have a root that expresses the connected meaning, but they may also have inflections (prefixes or suffixes) that alter the meaning. These inflections are connected to each other in the same network (Figure 3.3). These inflections are connected to other inflections in words that have unrelated meanings (Figure 3.4).

Inside this network may be noncontent words such as articles (*the, a/an*) that are connected to the types of words they can co-occur with. Thus, articles are connected only to words that can serve as nouns, and not to verbs or adjectives.

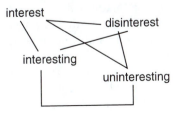

FIGURE 3.1 Connections for the word *interest*, based on root form and meaning

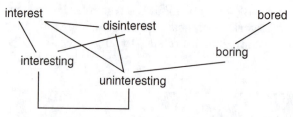

FIGURE 3.2 Connections for the word *interest,* based on semantic relationship

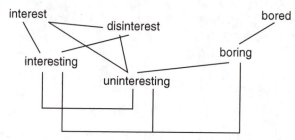

FIGURE 3.3 Connections between grammatical forms among semantically related words

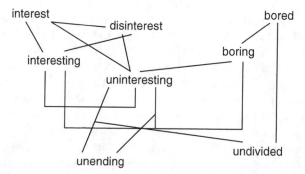

FIGURE 3.4 Connections between grammatical forms among semantically related and unrelated words

In short, the network is a vast map of lexical items and grammatical forms that are linked to each other via connections that demonstrate some kind of **semantic relationship** (that is, a relationship based on meaning as in *interesting* and *boring*), a **lexical relationship** (a relationship based on a root word's form, as in *interest* and *interesting*), or a **formal relationship** (a relationship based on grammatical form that doesn't change the meaning of the root but when added creates a new word, as in *boring* and *bored*). You can probably understand now why slips of the tongue happen. For example, have you ever said something like, "John told me all about his brother, I mean sister"? In such cases, people

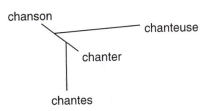

FIGURE 3.5 Lexical (root) connections in a French L2 learner's network

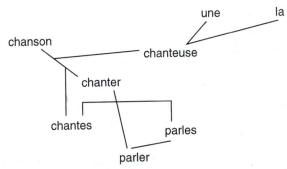

FIGURE 3.6 Lexical and formal connections in a French L2 learner's network

experience a temporary glitch in retrieving a particular word or form from this vast network and a connected item accidentally appears in speech when something else should.

L2 learners create similar systems. L2 words are connected based on semantic, lexical, and formal relationships. If we take the word *chanson* (song) in French, we would find it connected to words with the same root (Figure 3.5). These words in turn are connected to other words with which they may share formal (grammatical) relationships (Figure 3.6).

As with the World Wide Web, only a small part of the network can be rendered visually. For both the native speaker and the non-native speaker, the network consists of thousands and thousands of nodes with many more connections between them. This does not mean that an L1 network and an L2 network look the same; it means that both natives and non-natives create these networks based on the same learning processes.

Pause to consider . . .

the type of network just described. Take a word in your first or second language and list all the following that you can possibly think of. What does the list look like?

- semantic relationships
- lexical relationships
- formal relationships

The (Abstract) Syntactic System

Syntax, you may recall, consists of the rules that govern sentence structure. "What is possible (allowed) and what is not possible (not allowed) in a given language?" is a question within the domain of syntax. Some rules that govern sentences seem straightforward and easy to articulate. For example, one of the following sentences is not allowed in English. Which one and why?

(1) *Cat the sipped milk the.
(2) The cat sipped the milk.

The answer, of course, is that (2) is allowed and (1) is not. And the reason is pretty simple: Articles must precede nouns in English. (Articles also precede any modifiers of a noun such as adjectives, e.g., *the orange tabby cat* and not *orange tabby the cat*.) But what about the following sentences?

(3) My book is the one that Sarah stole.
(4) My book is the one Sarah stole.
(5) My cat is the one that scratched the sofa.
(6) *My cat is the one scratched the sofa.

In (4), *that* can be omitted in English and the sentence is fine. But did you have an immediate "Huh?" reaction when you read (6)? In (6), compared with (5), *that* can't be omitted. Why not? If you look at the sentences enough, you may see that in English you can delete *that* when it is an object of a verb in the embedded clause but not when it is a subject. (4) corresponds to *Sarah stole my book* whereas (6) corresponds to *My cat scratched the sofa*. But other aspects of sentence structure might elude you completely no matter how hard you tried to figure them out, or you might come up with an ad hoc explanation that would not satisfy a linguist. For example, what is a subject in English? Many would say, "the person or thing that performs the action." This is fine if the sentence has an action, such as *Mary kicked Bob in the shins*. Mary is the one who performed the action of kicking. But what of sentences such as the following?

(7) Mary likes Bob a lot.
(8) Mary seems tired.
(9) Mary got fired.

Clearly you know that Mary is the subject of each sentence, but your explanation can't be because she performs or performed some action. In (7) and (8) there is no action: *Likes* and *seems* are not like *kick, scream, write,* or *drive*. In these cases, Mary is actually *experiencing a feeling,* but in English we put her in subject position. And in (9), Mary didn't do anything but *something happened to her;* that is, she didn't fire anyone but someone fired her. So, what is a subject, then? Experts in syntax (again, the rules that determine sentence structure) would say that the relationship between a subject and a verb is a structural one and not a semantic or meaning-based one. Let's see how.

Syntacticians conceive of sentences as having hierarchical structure rather than linear structure. Hierarchical structure can be demonstrated visually by representing sentences as "trees." In the diagrams shown in Figure 3.7, the hierarchical structures of the sentences *Mary kicked Bob in the shins* and *Mary seems tired*

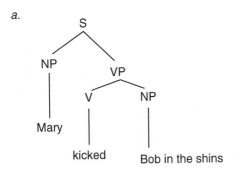

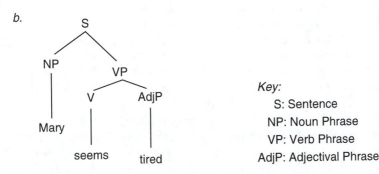

FIGURE 3.7 Hierarchical structures of the sentences *Mary kicked Bob in the shins* (*a*) and *Mary seems tired* (*b*)

are presented. (Linguists would represent these sentences a bit differently. We are taking some liberties to make the point as simply and clearly as possible.)

If you look at these two trees carefully, you will notice several things. First, the S is the highest entity in the tree. Second, there are always an NP and a VP that immediately "fall under" the S, or, as we say in linguistics, the S immediately dominates the NP and the VP. The VP in turn is higher up than a different NP ("Bob in the shins") in *a* and thus dominates it. The VP is higher up than the AdjP in *b* and dominates it. Now you already know that Mary is the subject of *a* and *b* and is an NP. You also know that Bob is the object of the verb in *a* and is also an NP. What distinguishes the two NPs in *a*, and what does the NP *Mary* have in common in both sentences? The S immediately dominates the NP *Mary* each time but does not immediately dominate the NP *Bob in the shins*. The VP immediately dominates the NP *Bob in the shins*. The conclusion is that in terms of a structural hierarchy, a subject is an NP that is immediately dominated by an S, and an object is an NP that is immediately dominated by a VP. Again, in current syntactic theory, the trees would actually be much more complicated and would show many more features of a sentence. The main idea is that the subject of a sentence is determined not by a semantic relationship to a verb but rather by a hidden and abstract hierarchical, structural relationship to a verb.

These abstract properties of syntax are what form the syntactic component of not only a native speaker's developing system but also a non-native's. These abstract properties are what inform us that a sentence is possible or not. To be sure, languages vary in terms of how certain properties work. These variations are called **parameters**. In some languages parameters work one way and in another they work a different way. English, for example, does not allow anything to come between verbs and their object noun phrases, as we can see with adverbs. French and Spanish do, however. (Remember that an asterisk means a particular sentence represents something not allowed in a language.)

(10) *John drinks often coffee.
(11) Jean boit souvent du café.
(12) Juan bebe a menudo café.

In at least one theory of syntax, the difference between English on the one hand and French and Spanish on the other is that a particular parameter functions differently in the languages. One of the jobs of L2 learners during acquisition, then, is to "set" the correct parameters in syntax for the language they are learning. We will consider this concept again later in this chapter.

To be sure, not every scholar of SLA believes in an abstract syntactic component such as the one we are describing here. Nor do they all believe that there are parameters and parameter "resetting" in SLA. However, we do know from research that L2 learners can make judgments about sentences that they could not have learned, practiced, or heard in the input (see Chapter 1). What is more, learners can often indicate what is *impossible* in a language. So, for the purposes of the present discussion, we are going to accept that learners have an abstract syntactic rule system that operates independently of the network of lexical items and forms (but they all exist within the umbrella concept of the implicit linguistic system). This syntactic system constrains sentence structure in the L2 just as it does in the L1.

Pause to consider . . .

the term *constrain*. What does this word mean? You might want to look it up in a dictionary if you're not sure of all its meanings. How else could you state that abstract syntactic rules *constrain* the possible sentences in a language?

Pragmatic and Sociolinguistic Competence

Having knowledge of a language also involves having pragmatic competence and sociolinguistic competence. *Pragmatic competence* refers to being able to infer meaning (i.e., what someone says) when something is not said. Examine this short conversation:

HARRY: Want to go to the movies tonight?
SAM: I've got an exam.
HARRY: How about tomorrow night, then?

Harry asks Sam a pretty clear question that is called a *yes/no* question in that Sam could easily answer yes or no. But Sam does neither. He says something else, and yet Harry knows that Sam is saying "No, I can't," as illustrated by the last line of the conversation. Harry is using his pragmatic competence to interpret Sam's statement. Here is another example.

> MARY: I am really freaking out about this interview.
> BILL: Why don't you do something to get it off your mind?
> MARY: Good idea. Wanna go shopping?
> BILL: Give me five minutes.

In this interchange, Mary expresses a concern that Bill reacts to with a "why" question. Normally a "why" question would illicit a "because" answer. (For example, Why does the moon revolve around the earth? Because of a force called gravity.) But Mary does not answer with a "because" statement. She correctly interprets Bill's statement as a *suggestion* and not a question. (In the last line, Bill actually uses an imperative structure. But is he really commanding Mary to do anything? What is the intent of his utterance?)

Conversations are full of interchanges in which listeners must use pragmatic competence to correctly interpret a **speaker's intent**. Like L1 speakers, L2 learners must develop this kind of competence if they are to be fully functional in a second language environment.

Sociolinguistic competence refers to the underlying knowledge that determines what is appropriate in a given context. Some languages, including Spanish, French, Japanese, and others, have different pronouns and verb forms that are used differentially depending on the person you're addressing (and in some cases, the person you're discussing). It is sociolinguistic competence that allows people to choose, for example, between *tú* and *usted* in Spanish, *tu* and *vous* in French, or a specific honorific in Japanese. But sociolinguistic competence also goes hand in hand with the kind of language you use with someone. Look at the following greetings. With whom would you use each and in what kind of circumstance?

- *Hey, how's it goin'?*
- *Hello. How are you?*
- *Good afternoon.*
- *Hi. How are you feeling today?*

As you pondered the above greetings, you thought about different kinds of people and their relationships to you. You probably considered whether you were very close to each person and, if so, just how close. You may have considered the context or situation and whether it was a formal one or an informal one. When you use language every day, however, you don't think about these things. You simply use language appropriately. Think of the following euphemisms for swear words. When would you use them and when would you use their actual counterparts?

- *Ah, shoot!*
- *Fudge!*
- *Darn!*

Children learning a first language may need to be told that something they say is inappropriate in a given context. The child who is corrected for saying a swear word in public is being taught a lesson in appropriate use of language. By the time they are adults, people have built up an implicit sense of appropriate use of language based on their cultures, subcultures, and family experiences.

L2 learners also need to build up sociolinguistic competence if they are to be fully functional in an L2 environment. Like L1 learners, they need lots of exposure to different contexts to learn how language is used. And like L1 learners, they may need to be told that something they said is inappropriate.

Pause to consider . . .

how pragmatic competence and socio-linguistic competence are acquired. Can they be taught? Or does the learner have to live in an environment where the language is spoken to acquire them? And what about dialects and regional differences? That is, French is spoken in Canada, France, and elsewhere. Does each area of the French-speaking world share exactly the same sociolinguistic competence? What about all the countries in the world where English is an official language?

To be clear, we have left out any discussion of phonological competence (the sound system). This is not because it is unimportant, as accented speech is a prominent feature of much of SLA. Compared to the other areas of language, L2 phonology is relatively understudied and there is not a lot to be said about it in an introductory book.

Do you remember what you were asked in the introduction to this chapter? What aspects of the L1 keep developing through adulthood? You were right if you guessed that what continues to develop for L1 speakers is the network of lexical items, in addition to both pragmatic and sociolinguistic competence. Throughout life we learn new words and throughout life we encounter new experiences in which we sometimes learn about appropriateness or how some speakers express particular intents.

HOW DOES THE SYSTEM CHANGE?

We have said several times that the learner's internal system is dynamic, meaning that it undergoes change (if the learner is constantly interacting with input). How does change come about? In this section, we briefly touch upon two processes that take place inside the developing system: accommodation and restructuring.

Accommodation

Have you ever heard the expression, "There's always room for one more"? Under what conditions would we say such a phrase? In any situation in which you have to make room for an unexpected person, you are said to *accommodate* that person. In a similar way, the developing system is constantly being asked if it can make accommodations for new linguistic data in the way of new form–meaning connections. What this means is that the system is being asked to place the new form into the vast network of lexical, semantic, and formal relationships described earlier—in short, to store a lexical item and any formal features associated with it. For example, a learner is listening to someone talk about her family. She mentions names and who they are. The learner hears a word several times and at first doesn't know what it means. Through context, the learner correctly identifies the word as meaning *brother-in-law,* and the lexical form becomes a candidate for accommodation. The system might first "pencil in" the new lexical form in a partial manner. That is, maybe only part of the word is penciled in. As the learner hears the word again in context and the form–meaning connection is once again made, perhaps another piece of the word makes its way into the system and the word is filled out in its entirety. In this case, accommodation happened in stages, from partial to full. Once accommodation is complete, every time the learner hears the word again, the form–meaning connection is simply strengthened (along with any other connections in the vast network that are related to it and relevant to the context in which it is heard). In this particular case, the word *brother-in-law* would become part of the lexical, semantic, and formal network of words and would be connected to other words such as *brother, sister-in-law, mother-in-law,* and so on.

Grammatical form can be, and usually is, accommodated in stages as well. Learners may pencil in only part of a form in the beginning. For example, in Spanish, regular simple past tenses take a strong stress on a vowel in the ending, such as *habló* for "he/she spoke." At first, the learner may pencil in only the vowel or only the stress, having to get the rest as the word or other third-person singular verb forms in the past are used. In Italian, the equivalent past tense consists of an auxiliary (either *avere* or *essere*) and a past particple. So, "he/she spoke" is *a parlato.* In this case, learners may first pencil in the *-ato* ending and not get the auxiliary. Their developing systems will accommodate the past tense in bits and pieces as learners are exposed to it over and over in the input. Again, once a form is completely penciled in, then subsequent exposure in the input strengthens the presence of that form in the network of lexical items and forms. The network created includes connections between the endings of verbs in the past tense.

As you may remember from Chapter 1, forms are not only lexical items and grammatical forms but also chunks of language. Learners may process phrases or whole utterances that appear frequently in the input and store them as such. For example, if a learner repeatedly hears "What's a . . . ?" in the context of asking for a definition, then that phrase may get stored as a chunk of language and may be connected to *what* in the network. The chunk does not consist of a word plus a contracted copula (i.e., the word *is* in its reduced form, *'s*) plus an article; it's simply one big "word," "whatsa."

Input processing is the initial stage of accommodation. Forms and meanings must be connected during comprehension to be candidates for accommodation into the network. The frequency of their appearance in the input also helps to determine how quickly the connections might be made and how strong the connections will be.

Restructuring

Reflect back to our analogy about the airline company as a complex system. Like a linguistic system, it consists of different components that together serve a common goal. What would happen, however, if one component of that airline company changed? Let's imagine that the company decided that to save money, it was going to reduce the number of flights by 20 percent. What are the repercussions of such a reduction? There is change at almost every level of the system. The number of flight attendants is reduced or their rotation schedules are radically altered. Pilot schedules are changed. Ground crews have to be shifted or altered in some way. Ticket selling changes. The list goes on. One decision or one change can cause a *restructuring* of the entire operation. There is a domino or ripple effect.

Restructuring occurs in linguistic systems as well. When a form or structure is accommodated, changes can take place in other parts of the linguistic system. Let's take a single example. Relative clauses in language can relativize different things (though not all languages relativize everything possible). That is, there are different types of relative clauses; a clause can show that a noun or pronoun is the subject of the verb in the clause, the object of the verb in the clause, and so on. Here are the possibilities for relative clauses using the relative pronoun *who*.

- Relative clause with *who* as the subject (S) of the verb: That is the man *who* stole my watch. (*Who* is the subject of *stole*.)
- Relative clause with *who* as the direct object (DO) of the verb: That is the man *who* I saw steal my watch. (*Who* is the object of saw, as in *I saw him steal my watch*.)
- Relative clause with *who* as the indirect object (IO) of the verb: That is the man *to who* I gave my watch. (*Who* is the indirect object of *gave*, as in *I gave my watch to him*.)
- Relative clause with *who* as the object of a preposition (Oprep): That is the man *about who* I told you. (*Who* is the object of the preposition *about*, as in *I told you about him*.)
- Relative clause with *whose* as the genitive (Gen) or possessive form: That is the man *whose watch* I stole. (*Whose* is the possessive or genitive form that indicates who the watch belongs to, as in *I stole his watch*.)
- Relative clause with *who* as the object of comparison (Ocomp): That is the man *who* I am taller than. (*Who* is the object in a comparative structure with *than*, as in *I am taller than him*.)

These six possible forms comprise what is known as a universal **implicational hierarchy** in languages for relative clause structure. We can visualize this hierarchy as follows:

$$S \longleftarrow DO \longleftarrow IO \longleftarrow Oprep \longleftarrow Gen \longleftarrow OComp$$

According to this hierarchy, if a language has any one of the relative clause types, it also has the ones to the left ("above"). Thus, if a language has OPrep clauses, the hierarchy says it also has S, DO, and IO clauses. If the language has OComp clauses, then it has all of the clauses. Conversely, if a language has DO clauses, this does not automatically mean that it has those clauses to the right ("below"). In short, the presence of a clause implies the existence of certain others; the hierarchy is unidirectional in terms of the implied presence of a structure.

Now imagine a learner of English who, in response to the question *Who's John?*, hears and processes, *You remember! John is the man whose car got stolen.* The internal mechanisms tag this structure as a Gen relative clause and conclude, "Aha! This language has relative clauses from S to Gen." The system then begins to restructure itself by now permitting all the clauses from S to Gen when previously it may not have had them all. This happens because the hierarchy is, again, implicational and this information is "in the minds" of every language user. Because Gen is lower on the hierarchy, once it is encountered in the input and is accommodated, it provides the learner's implicit system with a clue that other clause types must exist, that is, the ones above it on the hierarchy. As in the airline case, one change causes a domino effect in the system.

Restructuring can be a bit different from this example and involve much subtler properties of the syntax. Remember the discussion of parameters? Parameters are those aspects of the abstract syntactic system that vary from language to language. Language A may have a parameter set one way and language B another way. One such parameter is called the *verb-movement parameter*. In the theory of syntax that posits this parameter, words can move around in a sentence. Look at the following sentences:

> John said who is coming?
> Who did John say is coming?

Syntactic theory would say that the *who* moved from one position to another (and some other things have to happen because of the move, but they are not important to this discussion). If we sketched it, it would look like this:

> John said who is coming?

Some languages allow *Wh-* words such as *who*, *which*, and *what* to move, as in English. Others do not. Likewise, some languages allow verbs to move, but other languages do not. Compare the Spanish and English sentences that follow (*come* = eats). (Remember that an asterisk indicates an impossible sentence, one disallowed by the native grammar.)

(13) Juan come muchos chocolates.
(14) John eats lots of chocolate.
(15) Come muchos chocolates Juan.
(16) *Eats lots of chocolate John.
(17) ¿Come Juan muchos chocolates?
(18) *Eats John lots of chocolate?/Does John eat lots of chocolate?

Note how Spanish allows various word orders while English basically maintains subject-verb-object word order. ("Verb" here means a full verb or lexical verb such as *eat, run, sleep,* and *snore.* Auxiliaries such as *do, have, can,* and so on don't count. Thus, *Does John eat lots of chocolates?* maintains subject-lexical verb-object word order.) What syntacticians say is that Spanish allows verb movement (as do French and Italian, for example), whereas English does not.

Verb movement also occurs when certain adverbs are used. We saw examples of adverb placement earlier. Here they are again.

(10) *John drinks often coffee.
(11) Jean boit souvent du cafè.
(12) Juan bebe a menudo cafè.

In French and Spanish, (11) and (12) are permissible because the verb moves from a position between the adverb and object to another spot. (Within the theory, the verb *has to move* or the sentence is disallowed.) It looks sort of like this:

Juan a menudo bebe cafè.

In English, the verb can't move; the correct sentence is *John often drinks coffee*. In short, all languages have a "hidden underlying structure" and certain operations or rules are performed that move things around (again, depending on the language). In verb movement, the verb originates in a certain position but may get moved to another position and in some cases has to move to another position. So, the parameter for verb movement in Spanish and French is [+verb movement] ("plus verb movement") and in English, [−verb movement] ("minus verb movement").

Now suppose the developing linguistic system of a learner of Spanish does not have the parameter set to [+verb movement]. Maybe the developing system thinks the language is just like English. Then, early on in acquisition, the learner processes *yes/no* questions. In Spanish, such questions are largely structured as verb-subject-object (VSO), as in *¿Come Juan muchos chocolates?* The parsing mechanism notes this and delivers the information to the developing system. The internal mechanisms conclude, "Aha! This is a verb-movement language." As the hypothesis is confirmed by more VSO data, the system may restructure itself by switching to [+ verb movement]. Now, lo and behold, the system says that it is permissible to move the verb in front of an adverb so that subject-verb-adverb-object (SVAdvO) is allowed. The system did this not because SVAdvO was processed in the input; the system allowed a new structure because a parameter was changed that affected several sentence structures. This type of restructuring may occur slowly or quickly. Research so far suggests that it occurs slowly, but the possibility remains that the restructuring that results from parameter resetting could occur quickly. We simply haven't studied enough parameters in SLA to have sufficient evidence either way.

Several times we have said that the system concludes, "Aha!" The system doesn't actually say or do anything; the restructuring just happens. We use "Aha!" to underscore that a new piece of data has entered the system and the system has to do something with it. All restructuring happens outside of awareness. In the airline scenario in which one change causes change elsewhere, everyone is aware of the change; the change is a conscious one. With the developing linguistic system, changes happen and the learner does not know they are happening. It is, of course, possible to note a change after the fact. You may realize you are doing something differently than you did before or you may realize that you now know something you didn't know before. What is crucial is that you were unaware of the changes when they happened.

Pause to consider . . .

if you have ever had the experience of realizing that you knew something but didn't know you knew it. For example, have you ever said something in a second language and after saying it said something like this to yourself: "Where did I learn that? How did I learn to say that?" Or have you ever read something in your second language and after reading one particular sentence realized that you knew something about syntax you didn't know you knew?

If you are confused about the difference between accommodation and restructuring, you might use the following distinction to help clarify. Accommodation operates on words and forms; restructuring operates on sentence structure and the possible types of sentences in a language.

What we have discussed so far is summarized visually in Figure 3.8. First, the intake that is held in working memory becomes available for further processing. If new data are present and can be accommodated, then the developing system checks to see if they are relevant to a particular subsystem or rule within the grammar. If they are, then restructuring can be triggered.

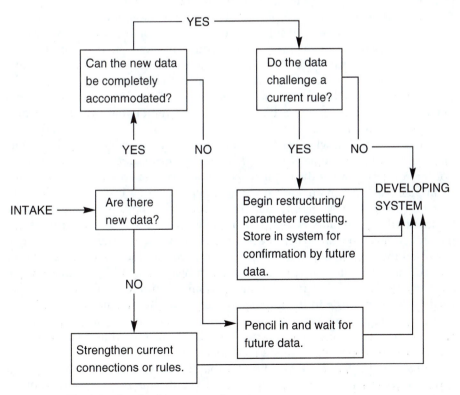

FIGURE 3.8 How the developing system changes

Up until now, we have described the developing linguistic system as implicit (as well as complex and in some cases consisting of some quite abstract rules and constraints). But many learners experience language learning under very explicit conditions, that is, they are taught rules, they memorize rules, and they practice rules. They learn rules such as, "In French, *de* and *le* contract to *du*," or "In English, –*ing* can be used to express immediate future events," or "In German, when you move an adverb to sentence initial position, the subject must go after the verb," or "In Japanese, all questions must be preceded by *wa*." These are examples of explicit rules that result in explicit knowledge in the head of the learner. These are not part of the implicit system as we have described it so far.

If explicit knowledge and the implicit system are different systems, several questions arise: (1) What role does explicit knowledge play in acquisition? (2) Does the explicit knowledge "turn into" implicit knowledge (become part of the implicit system)? There is still some debate on this matter in SLA circles, but there is consensus on the following: Without input, there is no acquisition, and input means only one kind of input, as we saw in Chapter 2. So, at best, explicit knowledge can play only a supporting or ancillary role. In a supporting role, explicit knowledge might help learners to process input better. In our model of input processing, for example, we saw that learners may use the first-noun strategy to interpret utterances and may get utterances wrong. If we explain to learners what this strategy is and that it may not work in the language they are learning and we provide examples, learners may be more inclined to be on the lookout as they process input subsequently. Research on this facilitative role for explicit knowledge is inconclusive; some studies find a positive effect for it and others find it contributes little if anything. But the possibility remains that explicit knowledge is beneficial, and a possible facilitative role should not be discounted yet. (In Chapter 4 we talk about explicit knowledge and output, and in Chapter 5 we touch on the role of explicit instruction and practice in learning another language.)

Does explicit knowledge "turn into" implicit knowledge? This is not the view that most SLA scholars would take. Being "facilitative" or having a "supporting role" in creating the implicit should not be equated with "turning into" an implicit rule. As an analogy, imagine a person with a broken leg who uses crutches. The crutches not only help the person walk, they also help to keep the leg immobile. Immobility is required (along with calcium and other things) for the broken bone to heal. When the leg is healed, we do not say that the crutches caused the healing nor that the crutches turned into the person's leg. We say the crutches facilitated the processes used in healing. In SLA, explicit knowledge may be used as a "crutch" under certain conditions while the processes used to develop a rule in the implicit system have their chance to work. And, as we will suggest in a later chapter, explicit knowledge may also *direct* learners' attention to things in the input they have missed, thus increasing the chances of processing those missed elements.

What is important to keep in mind is that the implicit system is built up via exposure to and processing of input and the subsequent accommodation of formal features that were attended to in that input. Restructuring may happen when certain forms or structures enter the system. Explicit knowledge is not input (you may wish to review this concept in Chapter 2), and so it cannot become part of the implicit system by the route we have outlined so far. Some learners, however, may learn a rule and practice it and use it well enough that it seems as though the rule has become part of the implicit system. Their performance is quick and seems effortless. This, however, is an example of a different process, as we discuss in Chapter 4.

SUMMARY

In this chapter we examined the nature of the network of connections that learners build between words and grammatical forms. As we saw, words can be connected because of meaning or because of root form. In addition, grammatical forms such as inflections and articles can be connected to the same forms on other words regardless of the connections among the words themselves. We also reviewed the abstract syntactic system, showing how implicit rules of sentence structure exist in both L1 and L2 speakers' linguistic systems. In addition, we touched upon the nature of pragmatic and sociolinguistic competence.

We also reviewed in some detail the nature of development in the linguistic system and how two processes, accommodation and restructuring, work to bring about change. Accommodation involves the incorporation of form into the linguistic system. Sometimes the incorporation is partial and sometimes complete. Restructuring refers to how syntax and other structures may change when the system gets certain kinds of data. These changes can create a ripple effect in which the data cause change somewhere else in the syntax (e.g., parameter resetting, implicational hierarchies), or they may be in evidence in U-shaped patterns of development.

Finally, we discussed the nature of explicit knowledge and its nondirect role in acquisition. Explicit knowledge does not turn into implicit knowledge, but it may be facilitative by getting learners to notice features of the input they have missed previously.

The implicit linguistic system develops slowly and requires much exposure to input. It is the system that the learner must ultimately tap into in order to create or produce language. Language production is the focus of Chapter 4.

READ MORE ABOUT IT

Networks

Bybee, J. (1991). Natural morphology: The organization of paradigms and language acquisition. In T. Huebner & C. Ferguson (Eds.), *Crosscurrents in second language acquisition* (pp. 67–91). Philadelphia: Benjamins. ▲

Elman, J. L., Bates, E. A., Johnson, M. H., Karmiloff-Smith, A., Parisi, D., & Plunkett, K. (1996). *Rethinking innateness: A connectionist perspective on development*. Cambridge, MA: MIT Press. ▲

The Abstract Syntactic System

Beck, M. (1997). Why syntactic theory? In K. Bardovi-Harlig & B. Hartford (Eds.), *Beyond methods: Components of teacher education* (pp. 42–66). New York: McGraw-Hill. [Very readable.]

Bley-Vroman, R. (1989). What is the logical problem of foreign language learning? In S. M. Gass & J. Schachter (Eds.), *Linguistic perspectives on second language acquisition* (pp. 41–68). Cambridge: Cambridge University Press.

Hawkins, R. (2001). *Second language syntax.* Oxford: Blackwell. ▲

Towell, R., & Hawkins, R. (1994). *Approaches to second language acquisition.* Clevedon, UK: Multilingual Matters. ▲

Pragmatic and Sociolinguistic Competence

Kasper, G., & Blum-Kulka, S. (Eds.). (1993). *Interlanguage pragmatics.* New York: Oxford University Press. ▲

Wolfson, N., & Judd, E. (Eds.). (1983). *Sociolinguistics and language acquisition.* Rowley, MA: Newbury House.

How the System Changes

Note: A variety of the readings in the various sections of Read More about It address how systems change in one way or another.

Beck, M. (1998). *Morphology and its interfaces in second language knowledge.* Philadelphia: Benjamins. ▲

Klein, E. C., & Martohardjono, G. (Eds.). (1999). *The development of second language grammars: A generative approach.* Philadelphia: Benjamins. ▲ [See Elman et al. (1996) under Networks for an alternative approach to the one in this book to describe both the implicit system and how it develops.]

Explicit Knowledge

Hulstijn, J., & Schmidt, R. (1994). Consciousness in second language learning. *AILA Review.* ▲

Krashen, S. D. (1985). *The input hypothesis: Issues and implications.* London: Longman.

Underwood, G., & Bright, J. E. H. (1996). Cognition with and without awareness. In G. Underwood (Ed.), *Implicit cognition* (pp. 1–40). New York: Oxford University Press. ▲

CHAPTER 4

Output

For many, the hallmark of language acquisition is speaking (or signing for those with hearing impairments). When someone asks, "Is she fluent in Chinese?" that person means, "Can she speak Chinese?" No one would take that question to mean, "Can she read a Chinese newspaper?" For children learning a first language, parents delight when children utter their first word, even though the child has been trying to make sense out of what others have been saying since birth. Humans even enjoy talking parrots, and dog owners love to teach Fido to "speak."

In this chapter we focus on this aspect of acquisition, that is, how L2 learners come to express themselves. One of the goals of the chapter is to show that separate processes are involved in speaking (or producing) language and that speaking is, in a sense, a by-product of acquisition. Let's start with defining the construct at hand: *output*.

WHAT IS OUTPUT?

How many contexts can you think of in which the term *output* is used? Look at the following items and consider whether you have heard or seen them used in some kind of conversation or text before.

- factory or plant output
- video or audio output
- a writer's output
- energy output

As you look back at the list (and you can probably add other contexts), you can get a clear sense of the meaning of *output*. Output refers to just about anything that emerges from something else, normally something that is purposefully produced. In SLA, **output** refers to the language that a learner produces; however, output is not just any language. In the introduction to this chapter, we made reference to talking parrots. But we know that parrots don't really talk.

They imitate speech, but they don't know what's coming out of their mouths (or beaks). They simply know that if they produce sounds in a certain way, they get rewarded.

Like parrots, L2 learners can imitate sounds and phrases; they can produce language and yet not know what they are saying. In an episode of the 1970s television show *M*A*S*H*, Hawkeye takes over an English class and gets a group of native Korean speakers to repeat after him, "Frank Burns eats worms." (Frank and Hawkeye did not like each other.) They repeat the words dutifully after him, but they have no idea what they are saying nor that Hawkeye is using them to make fun of Frank. This is not output.

Output, as we use the term, is not language production without meaning. *Output* in SLA means language that has a *communicative purpose*; it is language that learners produce to express some kind of meaning. It can be the output of an immigrant in a grocery store or bakery, an ESL student trying to register for classes in Kansas, a learner of German on a study abroad experience who is trying to buy a certain medication, a foreign language student in a classroom who is answering the question, "Who did you interview and what did that person say?", and so on. (There is also such a thing as written output, but writing and composition are the subjects of another book.) So, when we discuss issues related to output, we are speaking of the same kind of language that we speak of when we talk about input—language that has some kind of communicative intent.

Pause to consider . . .

why we might limit our discussion to communicative output only. Do you think the kind of language learners produce during drills is the same as the kind of language they produce when engaged in communicating an idea? Why or why not?

HOW DO LEARNERS MAKE OUTPUT?

When you speak in your first language, you have to do two things minimally: Think of what you want to say and then put that thought into speech (although you might be thinking that some people don't always think before they speak). L2 learners have to do the same, but they also have to learn how to do it. At least two processes are involved in *output processing: access* and *production strategies.* Let's look at each in turn.

Whenever you speak, you draw upon your vast network of lexical connections to retrieve words and forms to express a meaning. For example, if you want to express the concept DOG, you "search" your mental lexicon and access the word *dog*. If you want to express the concept FETCH, you access the word *fetch*. But you must also access grammatical forms. If there is more than one dog you also have to access the morphological inflection to express plurality, *–s* (as well as the phonological rule that makes it sound like the *z* in *zebra*). In short,

access refers to *activating the lexical items and grammatical forms necessary to express particular meanings.* In your first language, you access words rather quickly, in fact in milliseconds, so that when you speak you are thinking, accessing, and producing output all at the same time. You are producing something while at the same time accessing something that is coming next or later and also thinking about what needs to come after that. This ability is something that the L2 learner has to develop. We have all experienced either as learners ourselves or as instructors with our students that initially, learners produce halting speech, full of pauses, in an effortful search to access the mental lexical-form network to express a concept. (We discuss skill development later.)

But of course, in addition to finding the lexical items and forms, you also have to put them together in some kind of sentence or utterance. Here **production strategies** come into play. In your first language, these strategies are well rehearsed and you most likely speak effortlessly and easily. You have one set of strategies (actually, they are called mechanisms or procedures) and only one set. L2 learners, however, have access to two different sets. One they bring to the task of acquisition and the other they must develop. The former consists of the L1 production strategies and the latter of the appropriate L2 strategies. According to the particular theory in which the concept of production strategies has been developed, the actual procedures that underlie L1 and L2 production are probably the same. What the L2 learner does, it seems, is reconstruct the procedures with appropriate L2 rules and constraints.

L2 learners use the L1-based production strategies when they have not built up the appropriate L2 strategies and yet have to communicate beyond their current L2 abilities. In this case, the learner may access lexicon and form from the developing L2 system, but then use the L1 production strategies to put everything together. In a real sense, this is a **communication strategy**, a way of using what you know to express yourself when you really can't. The result, as many of us know, is something that sounds like the L2 but has the structure of the L1. A classic example occurs when English speakers learning French or Spanish attempt to express their ages. English uses *be* as the verb to express age whereas French and Spanish use *have* as the verb. Thus, learners produce *Je suis vingt ans/Yo soy veinte años* instead of *J'ai vingt ans/Tengo veinte años* to express "I'm twenty years old." In such cases, some might say the learner's L1 is "interfering" in the learning and that practice will help the learner overcome this. The problem may actually be that learners are simply asked to do something they can't, so they resort to what they can. Because the system has not incorporated a rule to express age, the learner generates a syntactic structure and inserts word equivalents between the two languages. Unlike children who are allowed to babble, speak in one- and two-word phrases, and so on, beginning L2 learners are often pushed (by themselves or those around them) to speak in larger phrases and utterances. The communicative pressure, in short, makes the output look the way it does.

L2-based production strategies must develop over time. How this happens is one of the least-studied aspects of SLA, but one theory has been articulated and enough research has been conducted to support it so far. This theory, called Processability Theory, hypothesizes that speech production rules or procedures exist in an *implicational hierarchy.* This means that some procedures must be in place before others can be acquired. Although we discussed implicational hierarchies in the context of change in the developing system in Chapter 3, let's review the concept here with an example from a physical activity: running. What procedures must be in place before a child can learn to run? Look at the following items and order them in terms of a hierarchy; that is, in terms of what must come before what:

- running
- standing
- walking

It is easy to see that a child must be able to stand before being able to walk and to walk before being able to run. The ability to perform one procedure *implies the ability to perform a previous one.* In the running scenario, the hierarchy would look like this, with "◄—" meaning that the procedure on the right implies the procedure(s) on the left: standing ◄— walking ◄— running.

In Processability Theory, six procedures exist in an implicational hierarchy. Here they are, with definitions and descriptions.

- *lemma access:* retrieval of words; basically the same as *access* (lemma is a technical term for "words"). This is the easiest of all procedures and implies no other preceding procedure.
- *category procedure:* use of inflections on lexical items. Here, the learner can not only access words but also put inflections on them, as long as the inflection is part of the meaning of the word and is not something that involves agreement with another word. For example, the learner can add *–ed* to *walk* to form the past tense, *walked.* Marking past tense is not dependent on agreement with another word; it exists independently of other grammatical items or words and is "fused" directly with the verb. Compare with the procedures that follow.
- *phrasal procedure:* use of inflections in a phrase. Now the learner can put inflections on words within a phrase, such as in noun-adjective agreement: *la casa blanca, la maison blanche.* The agreement is contained solely inside the noun phrase. (Subject–verb agreement involves a different procedure, as we will soon see.)
- *simplified S-procedure (S meaning sentence):* exchange of information from inside the sentence to the beginning or end of the sentence (usually the beginning). In standard word order in some languages we might say, "I talked to my mother yesterday on the phone." With the simplified S-procedure, you can "move" the adverb *yesterday* to sentence initial position, "Yesterday, I talked to my mother on the phone." You have moved it from somewhere inside the sentence to the beginning. This procedure also accounts for learners being able to use WH-questions in initial position when speaking; for example, instead of *You talked to who last night?* the learner can "front" the WH-word to make a more typical sentence: *Who did you talk to last night?* This doesn't mean all aspects of the sentence produced are correct; it just means that the learner can now move things around. In the last

- *S-procedure:* exchange of information between internal constituents, for example, between noun phrases and verb phrases. This procedure accounts for the ability to produce subject–verb agreement, among other things. Subject–verb agreement involves holding information about the subject (e.g., third-person singular, second-person plural) and "carrying" it over to the verb phrase to produce a correct verb form. Adjective agreement such as in *My house is the white one* in languages that have such agreement also falls under the scope of this procedure. The information about "feminine-singular" must be carried over to the verb phrase and used to correctly inflect the adjective, article, and in this case, noun: *Mi casa es la blanca.* As you might guess, if you compare S-procedure with phrasal procedure, it is easier to produce agreement "locally" in a phrase than to carry agreement across phrase boundaries in sentences.
- *subordinate clause procedure:* exchange of information across clauses. The most difficult procedure of all and the last to be acquired involves carrying grammatical or semantic information from a main clause to an embedded or subordinate clause. An example in Romance languages is the use of the subjunctive in embedded clauses. The learner must carry the information from the main clause that "triggers" the subjunctive into the embedded clause, so that the verb form gets inflected correctly. Subject–verb agreement across clauses also falls under the scope of this procedure: *John and Mary are the people who have yet to find a house.* In this example, the verb *have* must agree with *people.* (Note that even though we say *who* is the grammatical subject of the clause, it is used with both singular and plural nouns and does not indicate or carry number: *John is the man who . . . .*)

The hierarchy exists in the order the procedures were just presented, with lemma being the first procedure needed and subordinate clause procedure requiring the others that are listed before it. Remembering that our backward arrow means that the procedure on the right implies the ability to use the procedure(s) on the left, the hierarchy looks like this:

lemma ◄— category ◄— phrasal ◄— simplified S ◄— S
◄— subordinate clause

The theory says, then, that in speech production certain procedures must emerge and come under some kind of control before "later" procedures can be applied. (Remember that this is all happening moment by moment, and with fluency millisecond by millisecond.) So learners must first be able to access words before they can apply inflections to them, and they must be able to do these two things before they can apply inflections throughout a phrase that all refer to the same grammatical concept, and so on. You might understand a little better, then, why learners in the early stages produce words and two-word phrases but labor intensely to produce sentences. They are at the stage of learning to access the lexicon! You might understand also why something like the subjunctive is so difficult for early-stage learners of Spanish and French and why verb position in German main and subordinate clauses is difficult for first- and second-year students of these languages. If they are at the lemma and category stages of mastering the speech production procedures, we are asking them to produce utterances at stages far beyond their productive abilities.

If the L2 is English, the appearance of third-person *–s* in spontaneous speech would not happen until learners reached the processing stage of carrying grammatical information across or between phrases (the S-procedure stage). Attempting to have learners master this grammatical form before regular past tense forms, for example, is again asking them to do something that is beyond their processing abilities. Research applied to instructed L2 settings has confirmed that learners who have not built up the procedures required for a stage cannot move on to that stage during instruction. They might perform a controlled task in the short run, but their spontaneous output tends not to show ability to use what was taught. Learners can only move on to the next stage in the hierarchy for which they are ready.

It is important to point out here that in speech production models such as this one, no claims are made about the developing system. It is simply assumed to exist (in some form or another). Speech processing models are concerned only with how learners (or any speakers, for that matter) go about making output; they are not concerned with input or how learners create an implicit linguistic system. With this said, it is probably safe to assume that there may be some symbiotic relationship between the growth of the developing system and the emergence of the production procedures for learners. Think back to what we know about input processing, for example. Our first principles claim that learners pay attention to content words before anything else in the input. In early-stage acquisition, L2 learners are getting mostly words from the input; a lot of grammatical information isn't making its way into the system. At the same time, the production mechanisms are limited to lemma access. Thus, in a sense, the input-processing mechanisms and the output-processing mechanisms are working on the same things: lexical items.

The sets of processes and procedures involved in creating output are summarized visually in Figure 4.1. First, learners generate a message or thought. The access of appropriate forms and lexical items is then activated. As these

---

Pause to consider . . .

the role of L1 procedures in the development of L2 production procedures. Do you think they transfer over, or does the learner have to relearn procedures for a new language? As you think about this, note the following: Italian is a language rich in verb agreement such that in the simple present tense each verb form is unique to each person (unlike English). German is a language that has more verbal agreement than English, but it is not the case that each form is unique for each person as in the present tense in Italian. However, the research on Italian immigrant learners of German shows that they do not produce subject–verb agreement until they get to the S-procedure stage. What does this suggest to you?

67 ·

*What Is the Role of
Output in the
Creation of the
Learner's Linguistic
System?*

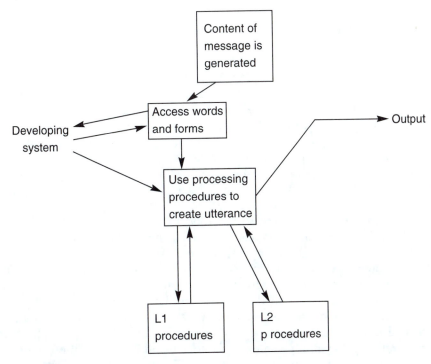

FIGURE 4.1 Basic processes in making output

forms and lexical items are accessed, production procedures (either L1-based or L2-based, possibly a blend at some times) are activated to put the items together in a serial manner.

WHAT IS THE ROLE OF OUTPUT IN THE CREATION OF THE LEARNER'S LINGUISTIC SYSTEM?

Have you ever studied a language in a classroom situation? Which of the following is the scenario of your experience?

- The teacher talked a lot in the second language. Our job was to listen. We didn't have to produce much.
- The teacher presented rules and then we practiced them with exercises.
- We learned rules but first got to see how they worked by trying to comprehend sentences before we were asked to produce anything.

Did you check the second scenario? If so, your experience is typical. Most people believe that the way you learn rules is by practicing them—and that kind of practice must be output practice. As we have seen, however, the developing system builds up as a result of learners' engagement with the input (plus other internal factors). In fact, as we claimed, every current theory in SLA posits some role for input as a critical ingredient in the entire process of acquisition. And as we saw in the previous section, Processability Theory focuses on the *procedures* required for making output and not on the *source of linguistic infor-mation* that the procedures draw from. So, is your language learning experience suspect? What is the role of output in the creation of the developing system?

There are three possibilities. The first is that output plays the same role as input. The second is that output plays no role. The third is that output plays a facilitating role. Before continuing, think about each possibility. What is your instinctive reaction? Check your response as we proceed with our discussion.

The idea that output plays the same role as input in the creation of a lin-guistic system is difficult to support. In any theory of anything, normally two different factors cannot play the same role. You catch a cold because germs enter your body. Only germs can cause a cold. Other things may help germs get into your body (e.g., not washing your hands) but these things don't actually cause the cold. SLA is like anything else, then; output cannot play the same role as input. And currently, there is no theoretical way to link output directly to acquisition. That is, we have established mechanisms for input processing and can articulate them to a greater or lesser degree. We have established processes that act on processed linguistic data so that the developing system can contin-ue to develop. These, too, are articulated to a greater or lesser degree. However, no theory to date has articulated any mechanisms that would lead output to provide data for the developing system. Again, as we saw before, the output processing mechanisms rely on or assume some kind of linguistic system for their operations; they don't create it. Our conclusion is, then, that output can-not play the same role as input; it cannot provide the data to the learner.

The position that output plays no role is equally problematic. Scholars work-ing in the area of interaction (learners speaking or interacting with speakers of the language) have offered some evidence that speaking promotes negotiation of meaning. As communication breaks down or clarifications are needed during a conversation, negotiation takes place. Such negotiations may put the learner in a position to notice something in the input he or she had not noticed before. Do you remember the interchange between Bob and Tom from Chapter 2? Bob and Tom played tennis on the same men's league and had the following conversa-tion one day in the locker room.

BOB: So where's Dave?
TOM: He vacation.
BOB: He's on vacation?
TOM: Yeah. On vacation.
BOB: Lucky guy.

As we commented in Chapter 2, this conversation shows that Bob's simple confirmation of what he heard (*He's on vacation?*) prompted Tom, the non-native speaker, to notice the preposition *on*. He went from *He vacation* to *on vacation* as he addressed Bob's confirmation request. By speaking, by engaging in some kind of interaction, Tom got something from the input. What these kinds of interactions do for learners is bring something into focal attention. Recall our discussion of working memory. Because Bob's meaning is not new (his question has a pragmatic function and is not really a standard yes–no ques-tion), Tom's attentional resources are freed up to notice a formal element of the utterance. Because Tom already knows what the meaning is, his resources for comprehension are just a little less taxed. This permits him to process just a little more language than he would otherwise.

Other scholars take the position that output can also encourage other processes that help learners acquire language, though they do *not* argue that output is data for acquisition. By being pushed to speak, learners may come to realize that they do not know something or that something in their systems is "fuzzy." The following interchange is one example. The two speakers are native speakers of English working out how the verb *sortir* (to leave, go out) works in French. Is it reflexive or not? They are talking about a mechanical arm coming out of a machine.

> s1: *Un bras . . .* wait *. . . mecanique . . . sort?*
> s2: *Sort,* yeah.
> s1: *Se sort?*
> s2: No, *sort.*

This interchange suggests that the learners have some kind of knowledge about the formal features of French. By working through an attempt to express meaning, S1 comes to see that something is not quite right in her system. The claim is that this particular interchange brings that to the learner's attention. By having heightened awareness, the learner may be more prone to notice instances of *se* in the input.

Another role that has been suggested for output in terms of the development of the internal system is that by speaking we may be forced to process input better. Note that the input processing strategies in Chapter 2 begin with a major principle, that the learner processes input for meaning before anything else. Why would learners process formal elements of little communicative value if they didn't have to? According to at least one scholar, knowing that you have to speak pushes you to pay more attention to what's in the input. If you never have to speak, you might be content with always processing the input only for meaning. But if you know that there will be production pressures on you at some point, you may become a more active processor of *how* something is said and not just *what* is said. This is called moving from purely **semantic processing** to more **syntactic processing** as you pay attention.

As we can see from this discussion, the current position is that output plays a facilitative role in acquisition, at least in terms of the developing system and its contents. This does not mean that output is not necessary. It is theoretically possible that some aspects of the input would not be processed or noticed if learners did not have experience making output. Making output may push them to be better processors of input, something they might not do otherwise. In this case, output may be necessary for continued growth. It is important, however, to note that we are not talking about learners *practicing* a form or structure in their output; we are talking about learners coming to the awareness that they need a form or structure because of their output. Input is still critical to how linguistic data get in the learner's head. Note how in the interchange between Bob and Tom, Tom said *on vacation* only because Bob said it before him. Bob's utterance was input for Tom.

Pause to consider . . .

the contrast between the facilitative perspective of output and the role that output plays in more traditional language classes. What underlying beliefs or assumptions about language learning exist for teachers who believe in traditional approaches to the classroom? Have your beliefs been altered by reading this far into this book?

HOW DOES SKILL IN SPEAKING DEVELOP?

Unlike the developing system, *skill* is not knowledge but ability. The fundamental factors that determine skill are *speed* and *accuracy*. You are more skilled if you are faster than someone else. However, your skill is better if you are also accurate while being faster. Do you know anyone who can type quickly? Does that person type without errors or does that person have to go back and edit a lot of mistakes? A skilled typist types quickly; a very skilled typist types quickly and makes few or no errors.

Skill development in speaking (actually, probably any skill related to language) is similar. When we talk about the speaking skill in L2 contexts, we talk about how accurate a person is and how much effort is exerted while speaking. This is called the person's **fluency**. Skilled or fluent L2 speakers are faster than unskilled speakers and may also not make the same errors. Native-like ability in speaking is considered to be something like fluid and rapid speaking ability with few or no errors (in any area of language—syntax, lexicon, pragmatics, and so on). We say that **automatization** has occurred when learners have reached such levels in making output, which translates into "speaking without much conscious effort."

Conventional wisdom would say that one learns to speak by speaking, just as one learns to tie shoes effortlessly by doing it every day. Put simply, speaking promotes speaking. But things are a little more complicated than that. Remember that learners have to be ready to use particular output-processing procedures and that they can't make use of ones they are not ready for. Thus, forcing people to speak beyond their current output abilities does little to foster either speed or accuracy. In a sense, skill development is incremental; learners gain control over the various procedures over time and each procedure needs to be developed. That is, each procedure develops in terms of the learner's ability to execute that procedure with little effort.

We also have to remember that Processability Theory and the procedures outlined in it address the creation of novel phrases and utterances. The theory makes no reference to the use of routines and unanalyzed chunks of language in speech production. Routines, as you may remember, are whole utterances that a learner uses in appropriate situations without having the utterance broken down into its components. Thus, "I dunno" could exist as a routine for a learner of English, as could "How do you do?" Prefabricated patterns are parts of utterances that are used in combination with other items to make sentences. Examples of prefabricated patterns are "Do you wanna _____ ?," *¿Cómo se dice* _____ (How do you say _?) in Spanish, and *Est-ce que* _____ ? to ask questions in French. The status of these prefabricated patterns and routines is not clear in native speech, although it seems logical that native speakers would have some of these, especially those that are frequent and well-worn in interactions. Some theories of fluency for native speakers posit that these chunks of language are important parts of everyday fluency. There is no reason to believe otherwise for L2 learners. With daily interactions in which routines and prefabricated patterns appear regularly in the input, learners may process them as such and store them as such. During speech production, they may call upon them in addition to the more word-by-word, creative aspect of speech production, just as native speakers do. Because these patterns and routines come out as chunks, learners may appear to be more fluent than they are compared to when they must create novel utterances. In any event, the point here is that not all production is word by word; not all production engages the production strategies and procedures we examined earlier. Some production involves the production of chunks independently of the use of the speech production procedures. Both aspects of production are involved in the development of speaking skill.

Currently, we have almost no SLA research on skill development in speaking. Although the idea that practice makes perfect (conventional wisdom) has intuitive appeal, we really don't know how L2 fluency develops and to what extent learners rely on chunks of language during production. We could turn to skill theories in cognitive psychology to look for possible ideas about how fluency develops, but more than one scholar has cautioned against wholesale importing of cognitive psychological concepts into language acquisition. If we believe that language acquisition is different from other kinds of learning, then we should research skill development in L2 speaking in its own right and not rely on models from other disciplines that research such skills unrelated to language. (We got into trouble once with behaviorism; "once bitten, twice shy," as the saying goes.)

Pause to consider . . .

why speaking might be different from other kinds of skills researched in psychology. Some of the latter skills are typing, performing alphabetic arithmetic (e.g., A = 1, B = 2, C = 3, and so on and then practicing computations such as B + C = ? and Z − T = ?), and detecting target letters embedded in visual displays full of distractors, among others. What makes speaking different? As you consider this, think about how language relates form to meaning.

WHAT ABOUT EXPLICIT KNOWLEDGE AND OUTPUT?

All of us backtrack and correct ourselves at one time or another while speaking. We say something like, "I talked to the telephone operation, I mean operator," and continue on. This shows that we are engaged in **monitoring;** if we realize something is wrong, we step in to fix it. We also monitor what we say before speaking to make sure it expresses exactly what we intend. Have you ever entered into a conversation with someone and deliberately spoken more slowly than usual because you were thinking, "If I say this, then he'll react this way. If I say this other thing, he may react differently"? These are examples of internal monitoring; the listener doesn't hear us doing it the way he or she would if we actually made a correction out loud.

L2 learners can monitor as well, but there is a fundamental difference. In L1 monitoring, we are relying on an unconscious and implicit system to monitor (except in those cases in which we consciously select *whom* instead of *who*, for example). When I make a mistake in speech, it is my unconscious system that is helping me monitor in my first language. L2 learners, on the other hand, can rely on explicit (conscious) knowledge to monitor their output. As they speak, especially under circumstances in which they are pushed beyond their internalized abilities and knowledge, we hear halting speech with lots of self-correction: "The man, he, uh, he, cut (pause), cutted (pause), no cut the tree." L2 learners know that they have explicitly learned and practiced something. They know they are supposed to use a rule in a particular instance. So they search out their explicit knowledge for the rule and apply it at the right time (or self-correct). Such monitoring is very typical of early- and intermediate-stage learners, and even advanced speakers may monitor for particular aspects of their output that they know they might not produce correctly. L2 learners can also monitor with their implicit systems once these systems are built up enough to be of use. In many cases, monitoring is useful as learners attempt to communicate beyond what their current implicit systems would allow. Monitoring "pads" their linguistic behavior and may allow them more interaction than they might receive otherwise.

Native speakers can monitor under just about any condition. L2 learners are more restricted. If there is pressure to just get the message out and not worry about it sounding completely right, a learner may not have the time to monitor. Thus, *time* is an important variable for monitoring. Accessing explicit knowledge and applying it take more time than accessing an implicit system. The latter is an effortful process. So, learners can monitor with explicit knowledge only if the task (time allotment) permits it. Also important is the obvious fact that learners have to have something to monitor with. Learners can monitor only if they *know a rule;* that is, the rule must exist either in their implicit system or their explicit knowledge. In Figure 4.2, we present a revised version of Figure 4.1 with monitoring added. Note the arrows that lead into monitoring; the monitor may rely on either implicit or explicit knowledge, as just discussed.

To be sure, a handful of scholars in language teaching believe that acquisition is the result of learners getting explicit knowledge in the form of rules and automatizing these rules through practice. In this framework, borrowed from

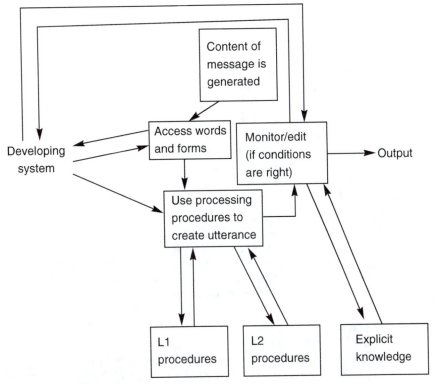

FIGURE 4.2 Processes in making output, including monitoring

work on skill development in general cognitive psychology, learners are said to begin with **declarative knowledge** about the language and then move to developing **procedural knowledge,** which is subsequently fully automatized. Declarative knowledge in SLA is usually associated with conscious knowledge, something that you have learned explicitly. It is sometimes referred to as "knowledge of" or "factual knowledge," such as "SLA stands for second language acquisition" and "Use *whom* instead of *who* after a preposition." *Procedural knowledge* refers to behavior and involves particular conditions that require particular actions. Automatization of procedural knowledge occurs when the person constantly performs the target behavior, in this case, speaking. So, for example, in making present tense verb agreement, a learner may start off with the declarative knowledge that when you talk about someone else, you must add an –*s* to the end of the verb in English. With some practice, this knowledge becomes proceduralized so that when the learner's utterance has produced a third-person such as *Gilbert* or *the dog,* an –*s* is added to the verb. As the learner converses more and more and must produce utterances about someone else, this proceduralized knowledge becomes automated. (Automatization implies, as you might guess, that someone does something with little or no effort, without thinking about it. It is important to point out here that practice does not mean drilling or conscious practice such as filling in blanks with verbs. Practice here means practice in communicating ideas, that is, talking about real things.)

Some kind of skill development may indeed underlie certain parts of an L2 learner's performance. If we think of skill development interacting with Processability Theory, we might say that once a speech-processing procedure emerges and allows learners to do something they could not do before, they have developed the procedural knowledge necessary to do that one thing. What they need now are opportunities to automatize the procedure via self-expression during communicative interchanges. In fact, in Processability Theory research, the evidence used for learners having moved to a new stage of processing is the *emergence* of certain aspects of grammar in their output, not their *mastery* of those items. Some kind of skill theory is needed to account for mastery in the output.

Many of us are quick to claim that the declarative $\longrightarrow$ procedural $\longrightarrow$ automatization account of language acquisition is how we learned a language. We first learned rules; we practiced them; and then we gained expressive control over them in our output. However, it is not feasible to think that advanced speakers of other languages actually acquired most of what they know and can do by moving from declarative knowledge to proceduralization of that knowledge. As we saw in Chapter 2, the best way to explain how we come to *know* more than we can *do* is through the internal mechanisms that interact with the data processed in the input. The implicit system contains far more information in the form of abstract rules than could have been gotten by proceduralization of declarative knowledge. In short, while skill development may be useful to help explain how learners learn to speak fluently and accurately, it does not address the matter of how learners create implicit linguistic systems. Once again, there is more to SLA than meets the eye.

SUMMARY

In this chapter we explored the nature of output and how learners develop the ability to produce language in speech. As we saw, output is language the learner produces that has a communicative intent. Learners must develop two important sets of procedures in order to produce such output: access and production strategies. Access refers to retrieval of lexical items and grammatical forms to express particular meanings. Production strategies describe how learners string the lexical items and forms together to create utterances. We reviewed one theory of such strategies, Processability Theory, that posits an implicational hierarchy for production strategies (actually called *procedures* in the theory). This hierarchy suggests that learners must develop procedures one at a time and in a particular sequence over time in order to use their implicit system for production in communicative contexts.

We also discussed the role of output in the development of the implicit system. Output does not play the same role as input; that is, by practicing a rule one does not acquire it. Instead, in communicative contexts, interaction with other speakers may allow learners to notice things in the input that they haven't noticed before, or the interaction may push learners to realize their system is missing something. Thus, output may play an important role but not a direct one in the creation of the linguistic system. Learners must still process input, and their internal mechanisms must still work on the processed input, in order for that implicit system to develop.

We concluded the chapter by reviewing the nature of skill development, focusing on a certain cognitive theory that hypothesizes movement from declarative knowledge to procedural knowledge to automatization of that knowledge. We mentioned that although there is probably some aspect of skill theory useful for describing the development of fluency and accuracy, we cannot use the theory to describe how the implicit system develops. What is more, we must also account for the possible use of explicit knowledge to monitor one's output. If the task situation is conducive to monitoring, then learners may edit their output as they go, drawing upon rules and forms they have stored in their explicit knowledge.

So far in this book, we have addressed the various components, mechanisms, processes, and learning issues in SLA that serve as the foundation for current research and theory development. We have asked the questions that researchers have asked, and we have summarized a good deal of SLA research in doing so. However, researchers' questions and instructors' questions are not always the same. In Chapter 5, we ask and answer common questions that instructors (and many laypeople) have about acquisition and teaching.

Pause to consider . . .

how and if you monitor in your second language. How effortful is it? Can you tell when you're doing it? What do you monitor for? Do you monitor by feel, using your implicit system?

READ MORE ABOUT IT

Making Output
Pienemann, M. (1998). *Sentence processing and second language development: Processability theory*. Philadelphia: Benjamins. ▲
Terrell, T. (1986). Acquisition in the Natural Approach: The binding-access framework. *The Modern Language Journal, 70*, 213–227.

The Role of Output in Acquisition
Gass, S. M. (1997). *Input, interaction and the second language learner*. Mahwah, NJ: Erlbaum.
Swain, M. (1985). Communicative competence: Some roles of comprehensible input and comprehensible output in its development. In S. M. Gass & C. D. Madden (Eds.), *Input in second language acquisition* (pp. 235–253). Rowley, MA: Newbury House.

Swain, M. (1998). Focus on form through conscious reflection. In C. Doughty & J. Williams (Eds.), *Focus on form in classroom second language acquisition* (pp. 64–81). Cambridge: Cambridge University Press.

VanPatten, B. (Forthcoming). The role(s) of input and output in making form–meaning connections. (Based on a plenary session delivered at the conference on Form–Meaning Connections in SLA, Chicago, February 21–24, 2002. Contact author for information.)

Output and Skill Development or Fluency

Schmidt, R. W. (1992). Psychological mechanisms underlying second language fluency. *Studies in Second Language Acquisition, 14,* 357–386. ▲

Monitoring

Krashen, S. D. (1982). *Principles and practice in second language acquisition.* New York: Pergamon Press.

Declarative and Procedural Knowledge

Anderson, J. (1995). *Learning and memory: An integrated approach.* New York: Wiley.

Dekeyser, R. (1998). Beyond focus on form: Cognitive perspectives on learning and practicing second language grammar. In C. Doughty & J. Williams (Eds.), *Focus on form in classroom second language acquisition* (pp. 42–63). Cambridge: Cambridge University Press.

CHAPTER 5

Frequently Asked Questions

In the previous four chapters we attempted to cover as much information as possible to give you, the reader, a view of the multifaceted nature of second language acquisition. At various times you may have stopped and either scratched your head or asked a question out loud because a particular aspect of a topic was not covered or what was covered made you think of something else. In this chapter, we have gathered together a variety of questions that teachers (and sometimes laypeople) often ask about SLA, in order to expand on the topics covered previously. Let's hope that all your questions are answered here!

DOES THE FIRST LANGUAGE CAUSE INTERFERENCE?

In the heyday of behaviorism in psychology and audiolingualism in language teaching, the first language was viewed as a problem to overcome. As we have seen, it was claimed that the learner transferred the habits of the first language into learning the second. As SLA research emerged, we began to see some interesting patterns. First, *the first language did not seem to affect acquisition orders* (Chapter 1). These orders were the same whether the first language was Chinese, Spanish, or Japanese, for example. In the research on developmental stages, again, *no matter what the first language was, all learners passed through the same stages* (Chapter 1). At the same time, we did see evidence of L1-like errors in speech. However, as we discussed in Chapter 4, learners may rely on L1 processing procedures to make L2 output if they must produce something beyond their current abilities; it is not that the L1 is influencing the implicit system, it is that the L1 speech procedures are a "crutch" for L2 production.

Today in SLA theory, **transfer** of the L1 is still debated, but the debate occurs in frameworks quite different from behaviorism. Some believe that the entire L1 system transfers and that it is the starting point for acquiring a second language (though it's not clear what this would mean for third or fourth language acquisition). In other words, the L1 generates the hypotheses about the

L2 that the input or intake data must eventually override. Some believe that only parts of the system transfer. Others believe that nothing transfers at the beginning but that transfer can be triggered by acquisition processes; that is, while learning a particular structure, learners may create a stage that resembles a structure in their L1. Those learners who do this may stay longer in this stage than learners whose L1 does not have a structure resembling the stage.

One of the clearest examples of this phenomenon comes from acquisition of negation. As described in Chapter 1, there are developmental stages in the acquisition of particular structures. In the acquisition of English negation, L2 learners are seen to pass through at least four stages, regardless of their L1. The stages are briefly summarized here again:

1. NO + verb phrase, e.g., *no drink beer*
2. subject + NO + verb phrase, e.g., *I no drink beer*
3. alternation of NO with DON'T, e.g., *I don't drink beer, He don't drink beer*
4. acquisition of *do* and correct placement of NOT, e.g., *I don't (do not) drink beer, He doesn't (does not) drink beer.*

German and Spanish make negation in distinct ways: Negation in Spanish is always preverbal with inflected verbs—that is, the negative is placed before the verb—while negation in German is postverbal with inflected verbs—that is, the negative is placed after the verb. (This is a simplification but all we need to illustrate our example of transfer.) Note that Stage 2 above resembles the preverbal negation typical in Spanish, whereas no stage resembles the postverbal negation typical in German. Spanish speakers learning English show evidence of lingering in Stage 2 longer than German speakers do, presumably because the resemblance of their L1 structure to the L2 stage triggers a transfer.

How we conceptualize L1 transfer depends, of course, on the kind of data we examine. As we have seen, speech output may fool us because we cannot determine whether the system has an L1-like rule or whether the learner is relying on L1 output procedures. Researchers who work within a syntactic theory framework (the kind we used in Chapter 3 to describe the syntactic component of the implicit system) often use grammaticality judgment tasks such as the examples given in Chapters 1 and 3. To examine the implicit system, they ask learners to make judgments about sentences to see what their internalized syntax looks like. Often the tests are constructed so that the sentences the learners have to judge are either L2 correct or L1-like in nature. For example, if we wanted to examine whether speakers of French learning English have discovered that English does not allow verb movement, we may use sentences such as *John likes not to drink a lot of coffee* as well as *John does not like to drink a lot of coffee* or *John drinks often coffee with cream* as well as *John often drinks coffee with cream*. The impossible sentences are based on the L1 syntax while the possible ones, of course, are not. Even in this scenario, it is not clear that learners use the L1 as the starting point or that there is transfer of some kind. A judgment task works fine for L1 speakers, but an L2 learner may not have a structure yet or may have reset a parameter. How does he or she judge the sentence? The only way possible is by relying on L1 rules. This is akin to relying on L1 speech procedures to make output. In short, what looks like transfer may be the result of task

79

*What about the Use
of the First Language
in the Classroom?*

demands; the learner renders judgments based on the L1 because there is something missing in the developing system.

To be sure, we all hear transfer in the sound system of learners. L2 learners are notorious for having accented speech (to greater or lesser degrees) and we can identify their L1s from their accents. But recall my Italian friend and the *cook/kook* distinction (Chapter 1). He could hear the difference but he couldn't produce it. Somewhere in his system he has acquired something about English vowels, yet his productive mechanisms can't access it. He relies on Italian articulatory mechanisms for pronunciation in English.

Even in input processing, the role of transfer is not clear. The first-noun strategy (Chapter 2) says that learners tend to tag the first noun or noun phrase in an utterance as the subject. Some have claimed that the results of the research on this can be interpreted as evidence for transfer because most of the research uses English-speaking learners of other languages. English is strongly subject-verb-object in structure, so the claim is that learners are transferring their parsing procedures. This may be so. At the same time, however, the world's languages are overwhelmingly subject-first languages; they use either subject-verb-object or subject-object-verb. Why would languages tend so strongly to have subject in first position before the verb unless the human mind somehow preferred it? Thus, the first-noun strategy could actually be a kind of universal parsing procedure and it could simply be coincidence that the bulk of the research uses L1 speakers of English.

The point here is that transfer is a slippery beast to research. We are limited in how we can examine whatever we examine, and whatever data we obtain can be interpreted in different ways. A commonsense conclusion from the research at this point is that transfer exists in some way for some things, but we have yet to pinpoint it exactly. Also, we have to distinguish between the transfer of systems and the transfer of processes or procedures as we conduct the research.

Pause to consider . . .

people you have encountered who speak your native language as an L2. How many of them sound native-like? Do they represent a range of abilities? Have you ever met anyone who was indistinguishable from a native speaker in terms of syntax and morphology (inflections) but perhaps had an accented pronunciation? Have you ever heard of someone who had flawless pronunciation but whose syntax and inflections were definitely non-native?

WHAT ABOUT THE USE OF THE FIRST LANGUAGE IN THE CLASSROOM?

Although everyone believes that teachers must use the L2 in the classroom to some degree, many wonder how much learners should use their L1 with each other in the classroom. Many foreign language teachers in the United States ask questions like this: "My students always use English when I put them in pairs. They don't practice the language as they should. Doesn't this hurt?"

There are two answers to this question. The first, of course, takes us back to input. As long as teachers are using the L2 as much as possible to communicate information and interact with classroom learners, they are providing input for acquisition. In addition, as we have seen, learners' output does not directly lead to acquisition of the implicit system, although it may be beneficial and sometimes necessary to force learners to see things they have missed or don't quite have down yet. So, as far as the acquisition of the system is concerned, learners' use of English (or any L1) in tasks is not a major problem in foreign language classes in terms of inhibiting acquisition.

But as we have seen, speech production is necessary for the development of L2 output procedures as well as for the development of skill. Does using the L1 interfere with the development of this process? Let's first ask why learners may be using the L1. Learners may use the L1 because they have not built up the output processing abilities to perform the tasks demanded of them. That is, the tasks require them to produce language beyond their capacity. They may also use the L1 because they are trying to get a fix on the task and to seek clarification from their classmates. So, perhaps it is the tasks that are the problem and not the use of the L1.

The second answer to the question involves research on the use of the L1 in tasks and what happens over time. Some insightful research has shown that as learners gain familiarity with a task, their use of the L1 drops dramatically. Other research shows that use of the L1 simply dissipates as learners gain successive control over output in the L2. What this research suggests is that use of the L1 may not be a problem in the early stages but may actually be useful if not necessary as a tool for learners to manage their environment and learning tasks. As learners gain control over productive use of the L2, they are increasingly able to use it as a management and learning tool. Until they are comfortable doing so, use of the L1 will appear.

Pause to consider . . .

why for some if not most teachers the use of the L1 by students in the class- room is an issue. Where does this concern come from?

IS SLA LIKE FIRST LANGUAGE ACQUISITION?

This question has been at the heart of SLA for decades, even before the contemporary era of actual empirical research on both L1 and L2 acquisition began in the 1960s. The answer is neither "yes" nor "no" but rather "it depends on what you look at."

L1 and L2 acquisition look the same from the outside when we consider the following:

- Both require communicative input;
- Both exhibit acquisition orders and developmental stages (which overlap considerably);
- Both exhibit growth from one-word utterances to phrases to sentences;
- Both seem resistant to external manipulation (overt teaching, overt correction) and essentially follow their own courses of development (more on that in a later FAQ).

L1 and L2 acquisition look different from the outside when we consider the following:

- L1 learners acquire an implicit system completely; few L2 learners do;
- There is considerable individual variation in how far L2 learners get, but there is almost complete uniformity in L1 acquisition (under normal circumstances);
- Although many errors and patterns of development are similar if not identical between the two, some errors are unique to one or the other context;
- L2 learners already have one linguistic system; L1 learners do not.

The question then becomes, To what are the differences attributable? If there are differences, then must the processes underlying each be different? Not necessarily. Remember that our claim is that SLA processes do not change because of context: Foreign language learners, immigrants, and L2 learners all must make use of the same processes if they are ultimately to be successful (relatively speaking). Differences that surface in these contexts could be attributable to cultural factors, task demands, availability of input and interaction, and numerous other factors. It is possible, then, that the differences we see between L1 and L2 acquisition are also attributable to external factors and not to internal processes. If you stop to think about the fact that a child spends the first five years of life doing nothing but playing and interacting, it's no wonder language acquisition happens. Adults and adolescents would have to be immersed for tremendous amounts of time and interact one-on-one constantly in the same kind of linguistic contexts (play, storytelling, clothes changing, bathing, mealtime, and so on) to receive the same kind of linguistic input and interaction that children do. And imagine what would happen to the L1 child if the task demands placed on adult L2 language learners were applied: speak in complete sentences, talk about the past the minute you learn about it, talk about abstract concepts, listen to a news broadcast and take notes, and so on.

In addition, many adolescents and adults are resistant to acquisition. Many come to the task of language learning thinking they can master it the way they master math, woodshop, or interior decorating. If you put your mind to it, study, and practice, you'll get it. This kind of approach demonstrates learners' lack of understanding of the nature of SLA and may actually interfere with the process.

Pause to consider . . .

the following statement: *Two activities can utilize (essentially) the same processes but result in different products.* Does the statement make sense to you? If so, can you think of examples other than language acquisition for which this might hold true?

DON'T IMITATION AND REPETITION PLAY A ROLE IN ACQUISITION?

This question reminds me of a story an SLA colleague told me about her oldest child. He was to go to Italy with his father for the summer and was concerned that he wouldn't be able to talk to anyone. My colleague told him that she and her husband would start speaking to him in Italian and would spend more household time speaking Italian. He looked at her, concerned, and said, "But that's not the way we learn languages. You say something and I'll repeat it after you." And he was only seven years old.

My colleague's child showed evidence of already believing things about language learning that adults believe. In Chapter 4, we mentioned the episode of *M*A*S*H* in which Hawkeye has a Korean EFL class doing choral repetition of "Frank Burns eats worms." Do imitation and repetition help? If they don't, where does this idea come from? Let's take the second question first.

The idea that imitation and repetition play major roles in language acquisition comes from two sources. One is the perception that adults have of how children learn their first language. Although it is true that children imitate and repeat, the amount of imitation and repetition they do is really rather little. Parents try to get their children to repeat *mommy* or *daddy* to them (in some families it is a race to see which word the child utters first!) and they delight when the repetition happens. The emotional impact of that repetition colors the parents' perception of acquisition. (By the way, in the race for *mommy* and *daddy*, the mom usually wins, but not because the child repeated what the mother asked him to. The *m* sound seems to be the universally easiest consonant to produce for children, along with *b*, and the vowel sound *ah* is also the easiest vowel. The child is not repeating; the child is simply saying the syllable that he would have said first anyway: *mah*. Sorry, moms.)

Children also play language games in which they repeat sentence after sentence, but these are games and not part of interactions. If a child is repeating sentence after sentence, the child can already produce that sentence. She didn't learn it by imitating and repeating it. (Again, this is not to say that imitation plays no role in child language acquisition; it just doesn't play the role people think it does and certainly doesn't play a major role.)

The other source for people's beliefs about imitation and repetition is past experience in language learning. Because of behaviorism's marriage to language teaching and the subsequent birth of audiolingualism, pattern practice became a staple in language teaching. Teachers were trained in special techniques to get learners to imitate and repeat. Even with the demise of audiolingualism, pattern practice has lingered on long past its usefulness. In 2001, I sat in on a workshop in which a graduate student supervisor demonstrated a lesson in a language the participants did not know. Part of her technique was to have students repeat after her. Airline flight magazines abound in ads for crash courses in other languages. Most of these self-teaching programs involve repetition; in fact, one company advertises with the following slogan: "Learn languages easily the way you did your first language. Just listen and repeat."

So, we have been trained by our environment to think that repetition is a major if not necessary component for successful language acquisition. Interestingly, some of these programs may provide results. People can get around in another country after they take these courses. However, this ability does not occur because imitation and repetition foster language acquisition. If learners are attending to the meaning of what they are supposed to imitate, then they are getting a kind of input. Even though their job is to listen for the purpose of repetition, some learners in such programs like to know what they're repeating. By attaching meaning to the utterance they are going to imitate, the learners are engaged in making form–meaning connections to a certain degree. Just as important is that such practice fosters an explicit system as well. And learners can function quite well with a limited explicit system that is well rehearsed. However, if they get into a situation for which they have not practiced the patterns, they are literally at a loss for words—as most L2 learners who have had this experience report.

As one final point, let's remember what repetition develops: the ability to perform a particular task quickly. If the task varies, the ability slows down or disappears. With language, you can learn sentences and produce them well through repetition. What you can't do is create with language, that is, participate in conversations. A friend of mine prides himself on his ability to remember dialogues from high school Spanish and French and is always telling me he can speak these languages. At times he has burst into a memorized dialogue in French. One day I decided to switch to French during our dinner conversation. After two minutes he said, "Let's go back to English." So much for repetition fostering acquisition.

Pause to consider . . .

the practice of repeating phone numbers out loud. Some people, for example, say that repeating a phone number helps them to remember it as they go to dial it, but many also report that once the number is dialed and the conversation is completed, they don't remember the phone number. Why do you think this happens? Can you think of counter examples in which the information "sticks" after this repetition? That is, in what domains does repetition actually help the long-term storing of information? Are these situations different from language acquisition? If so, in what ways? Are they similar in any ways?

SO DRILLS DON'T HELP, THEN?

Three kinds of drills are used in language teaching: mechanical, meaningful, and communicative. Two variables distinguish them from each other. The first variable is whether the learner has to pay attention to meaning to perform the drill. The second is whether the learner has any control over the response, that is, whether there is one and only one possible correct response. On mechanical drills, the learner does not have to pay attention to meaning and has no control over the response. Examples include repetition, substitution (in which learners are given a word and must put the word into the sentence and make any changes, often used for practicing verb forms), and transformation (in which learners change one structure to another, for example, changing actives to passives). The learner does not have to pay attention to meaning to perform the drill. This is easily demonstrated when we substitute nonsense words into a mechanical drill. Learners can still do the drill. At the same time, there is only one correct response and the instructor knows what it is.

Meaningful drills are those in which the learner still does not have control over the answer but does have to pay attention to meaning. Typical meaningful drills are those in which the learner has to answer a question to which everyone knows the answer. Let's say you want to practice contracted *is* with *it* so that learners have to use *it's*. For example, a teacher might ask "Where's the clock? Where's the desk? Where's the blackboard?" and so on. Learners' responses are, "It's on the wall. It's over there. It's _____." But the locations of all these objects are known by everyone, and the learner has to say the right thing or else the response is wrong.

Communicative drills are those in which learners must attend to meaning and are freer to respond. The instructor and other students may not know what the answer is. For example, if a class is practicing third-person *–s* in English, the teacher might ask questions such as "Where does your father live? Where does he work?" and so on. Although responses require "lives," "works," and so on in them, the instructor does not know where the father actually lives or works. The response is thus in the control of the learner.

The first thing to notice about drills is that they are output-oriented. They require learners to produce. So, to the extent that drills attempt to get learners to acquire the very thing they are asked to produce, the cart has been put before the horse. That is, there is no input for learning here. Acquisition of third-person *–s* comes from hearing and processing it in the input. Production of it comes from having acquired the appropriate output procedures for the L2. Learners are being asked to do something before they have undergone acquisition. The second thing to notice is that mechanical drills do not require attention to meaning. If you aren't attending to meaning, you aren't engaged in comprehension (putting aside the fact that drills are output-oriented anyway).

Research conducted since the early 1990s has shown that traditional approaches to teaching grammar that involve the use of mechanical, meaningful, and communicative drills do not foster acquisition in the way that practice with "structured input" does. (Structured input is described later in this chapter and again in the Epilogue.) In these studies, learners either receive traditional instruction or they receive **processing instruction** that involves having them respond to input sentences (they don't produce during the instruction).

The input sentences are structured in ways that discourage input-processing strategies that aren't conducive to acquisition. All of these studies report that the processing instruction results in improved performance on both interpretation and production tasks. (Processing instruction is discussed more fully in the Epilogue.) The traditional instruction results only in production ability (learners still don't interpret sentences correctly after the treatment). Thus, the drills in the traditional instruction weren't doing what many thought they were. Learners were imitating sentences and getting explicit knowledge, but the instruction was not affecting their implicit systems.

Pause to consider . . .

the different kinds of drills or practices mentioned in this section: mechanical, meaningful, and communicative. Do you know of any other such hierarchy in learning anything else? For example, does such a hierarchy exist in learning sports? How do you learn to play a sport? Do people learning a musical instrument have different kinds of practices? Do you think that learning to play an instrument is like learning a language?

DO LEARNERS DEVELOP BAD HABITS IF THEY AREN'T CORRECTED?

The concept of bad habits stems from the days of behaviorist approaches to language acquisition. Learners came to the L2 with L1 habits that needed to be suppressed. Activities were to be constructed so that errors would not be induced. If errors did arise, they were to be corrected immediately and appropriate practice engaged. The idea was to avoid the development of bad habits.

In SLA theory, there exists a construct called **fossilization.** This term refers to arrested development, the process by which a learner plateaus or stops learning. What is different from the behaviorist idea of bad habits is that fossilization—though not desirable and certainly not anyone's goal—is taken to be something that just happens and that may be unavoidable for some learners. Not everyone fossilizes on the same rule nor do entire systems fossilize in the same way. And from the presentations in Chapter 4, you might guess that fossilization in the development of speech procedures is different from the fossilization of the implicit system or any rules it contains. Several famous cases of fossilization have been presented in the SLA literature. All cases have involved L2 learners in more or less natural environments, some having received instruction and some not. Attempts at remediation had no effect.

What is clear from the research on error correction and development is that correction in the form of **overt correction** does little good in the long run. Overt corrections include any conscious drawing of attention to the error and (normally) how to "say it right." Overt corrections might cause temporary improved performance (the learner may monitor more because the overt correction establishes or reinforces conscious knowledge), but they don't cause an actual change in the underlying implicit system and they don't cause lasting changes in the output-processing procedures. **Indirect correction** may be useful. Indirect corrections are those that are part of a communicative interchange in which attention is drawn not to the error per se but either to the communicative intent or to the information the learner is attempting to convey. These corrections include recasts and confirmation checks, in which a speaker rephrases what a learner says (to see if the speaker heard correctly, to verify a point, etc.). Remember Bob and Tom, the tennis players. Bob performed an indirect correction when he recast Tom's utterance and included the missing preposition. As we saw, these recasts can serve as additional input; since the learner does not have to expend a lot of energy to comprehend the message, a form or structure may "pop out" in the input and push acquisition along.

Pause to consider . . .

what happens in natural conversation between a language learner and a native speaker. What does the native speaker attend to—what the learner says or how he or she says it? That is, does the speaker *overtly comment* on the grammaticality of the learner's utterance or does the speaker overtly address something else?

DOESN'T GIVING LEARNERS RULES HELP? (THAT'S THE WAY I LEARNED.)

This question is one of my favorites. Because we as language teachers are more successful at language acquisition than much of the population (in the United States, anyway), we think that how we learned is the way languages are learned. But once this idea is examined carefully, it begins to erode. Language teachers who are advanced speakers generally have gone abroad. The most advanced speakers have lived abroad or traveled extensively, listen to music in the L2, watch movies and TV in the L2, and so on. What do these situations have in common? Either lots of input or lots of input and interaction. Teachers think that because they may have learned rules first, these rules either caused acquisition or became the implicit system. We've dealt with this issue several times in this book and briefly repeat an important point here: You can't know what you know implicitly in an L2 or perform in an advanced manner if all you did was get rules and practice them.

But let's look at some empirical facts. In some research on instructional efforts, learners who are given rules outperform learners who aren't given rules. The latter learners are either in control groups (who get nothing) or groups who get some kind of practice but no preceding rule. Other research, however, has shown that getting rules is not what makes a difference; it is the practice that makes the difference. In these latter studies, the practice is of a particular kind called **structured input**. Unlike other instructional approaches, the approach that uses structured input actually attempts to alter learners' input-processing strategies (see Chapter 2). The other approaches do not.

87

Doesn't Giving Learners Rules Help? (That's the Way I Learned.)

We review structured input in the Epilogue, but for illustration's sake, let's examine the first-noun strategy, in which learners tend to process the first noun or noun phrase they encounter as the subject of the sentence. Learners of English may process passives as actives and incorrectly interpret *Mary was corrected by John* as *Mary corrected John*. Structured input would include activities in which learners might hear active and passive sentences mixed up and have to identify which picture goes with which sentence. When they hear *Mary was corrected by John* and they incorrectly select the picture of Mary correcting John rather than the picture of John correcting Mary, they get feedback that it's the other picture that represents the action. Their internal processors are forced to reevaluate the first-noun strategy as they encounter more passives in these activities. In this sense, acquisition is failure-driven: "The way I am processing this input does not match the meaning intended by the speaker. My processing fails me. I need to adopt other ways of processing the input." Structured input facilitates this kind of reevaluation. Maybe the equivocal results of the research mentioned at the beginning of the previous paragraph point not to a problem of getting rules versus not getting rules but to whether the activities provided with the rules actually work on processes known to be part of the acquisition of another language. Structured input works on these processes. It is not clear that the activities in other kinds of approaches do.

Ultimately, however, the matter does come down to, "How can learners know more or do more than they were taught and have practiced?" They can do this only if acquisition is driven not by explicit rules but by interaction with input data. Explicit rules can serve a useful purpose in the early stages, as we saw in the case of monitoring. The rules allow learners to perform beyond their competence, something quite useful in communicative situations if time allows it. But monitoring is not acquisition; it's one way in which learners make output. So rules don't lead to acquisition; they lead to explicit knowledge that may be tapped for communicative purposes if a learner can monitor. The illusion for some is that because the rule came before the input, the rule caused the acquisition or became part of the system. A better explanation is that the rule helped the learner to perform certain tasks while the system was building up via the regular channels of acquisition.

Some scholars maintain that explicit rules may be useful not because they help learners produce output but because they sensitize learners to input. The claim is that knowing something is out there in the input may make it more salient, that is, make it more likely to be perceived and processed. This is certainly a viable claim. However, we have yet to see research on the claim, so for now it remains a hypothesis.

Pause to consider . . .

what happens to explicit knowledge over time. Can you remember, for example, formulas for chemistry from high school? Any geometry proofs? Why did you learn these things, and if you don't remember them, why not?

SO DOES TEACHING MAKE NO DIFFERENCE?

This question is often asked of SLA researchers when they make presentations to language teachers. It is certainly understandable that if you dedicate your life to language teaching and it is something you enjoy, you might be discouraged by the results of SLA research. But there is another way to ask this question that makes better use of the research: What can teaching do and what can't it do? And let's be clear: The question is about explicit teaching and practicing of rules, not about language teaching in general, as long as language teaching involves more than the presentation and practice of rules.

What can't teaching do? It can't alter acquisition orders. It can't make learners skip developmental stages. It can't influence how the developing system creates a syntactic component. It can't make learners skip stages in the acquisition of output procedures. In short, it can't change any of the inherent processes in SLA. For example, one study reported the effects of intensive practice on a certain form in English by native French speakers in Canada. The practice disrupted the acquisition order. However, within a year the learners were back to where they had been before the intensive practice, and the acquisition order "reasserted" itself. In this case, the teaching delayed the natural path of the learners.

What can teaching do? Although we address this question more fully in the Epilogue, the brief answer is that teaching can be beneficial. First, it may heighten learners' attention to things in the input they might miss otherwise or might get wrong (e.g., make the wrong form–meaning connection). The result is that acquisition is speeded up. Second, classrooms tend to have richer and more complex input than a lot of naturalistic environments. Compare, for example, classes in which learners are exposed to stories and essays. How does this input compare to what immigrants might experience? The result is that classroom learners may not only go down the acquisition path faster, they may also get further. To be sure, these findings are tainted by motivation and socio-economic issues (e.g., educated college students vs. working-class immigrants who may even be illiterate), but they are suggestive.

Some strong emerging research suggests that *type* of teaching may make a difference. We touched on this in a previous section when we discussed traditional instruction, and we address this matter again in the Epilogue.

Pause to consider . . .

how you might discuss or recast the relationship between instruction and acquisition. Two possibilities are *Instruction is limited* and *Instruction is constrained*. Although close in meaning, they do not represent exactly the same concept. Which do you think represents best what you have read so far? Can you think of some other way to conceptualize the effects of instruction on acquisition?

ARE SOME LANGUAGES MORE DIFFICULT TO LEARN THAN OTHERS?

This is an interesting question. I often hear English speakers say that Russian is difficult and Spanish easy. I sometimes hear speakers of Spanish say that English is a difficult language. These comments are largely based on classroom experiences, which hints at an underlying issue in the question, but they may also reflect language acquisition experiences outside the classroom. Before discussing the question, let's look at L1 acquisition. Are some first languages more difficult for children to acquire than others? In the field of L1 acquisition, it makes little sense to talk about some languages taking longer than others to acquire. The reason is that if a language had so many features that it took a long time to acquire, children would eventually "fix" this problem in language acquisition. (This is essentially how languages change over time, by the way—through child language acquisition.) Over time, the hard parts would be disassembled so that children could acquire the language in a reasonable period of time. Remember, languages are organic entities subject to change. Languages tend to balance themselves so that if one component is somewhat difficult, other components are easy. In this way, languages always remain in an optimal state for acquisition. A colleague in child language acquisition had this to say to my question about language difficulty: "Every language has some things that kids get right away and other things that even school-aged kids mess up, but as a whole no language can be considered easier or harder."

In SLA some evidence has been reported that it takes more hours to learn certain languages than others. The Foreign Service Institute (FSI) reports that it takes more hours for English speakers to reach a certain level of proficiency in Russian than in Spanish. This evidence would certainly suggest that some languages are more difficult to learn than others. However, these figures are based on classroom learners' acquisition of language and are influenced in part by factors outside the internal processors responsible for language acquisition. For instance, classroom learners spend time becoming literate in the L2. Since Spanish shares an alphabet with English but Russian does not, it takes more time to master the alphabet, learn how to spell, and so on, in Russian. In addition, classroom language experience involves explicit instruction in grammar. The Russian inflection system is more complicated than the Spanish system, and instructors may spend extra time on the overt teaching of this system, thus lengthening the acquisition experience. More important, however, is the fact that the proficiency measures are based on an FSI scale of oral ability. As we saw with output-processing procedures, learners may fake their oral ability by using their L1 procedures. Since Spanish resembles English more than Russian does, L2 learners of Spanish may exhibit a higher level of proficiency earlier than L2 learners of Russian, who, if they rely on their L1 procedures, will sound much less native-like. We have no idea what these learners' internal representations of the language look like, nor do we know to what degree they have acquired any of the output procedures for the L2.

By making this argument, however, we are not discounting the possibility that some languages may take more time to acquire than others. We are simply underscoring that how we measure acquisition and what we measure need to reflect the totality of acquisition. Otherwise, we may wind up fooling ourselves that learners either know and can do more than they can or vice versa—that they know and can do less. In the case of Russian versus Spanish, Russian may indeed be more difficult than Spanish, but that is mostly in the initial stages. It is not clear, for example, to what extent cognates in aural input (words that sound alike in different languages and mean basically the same thing) facilitate acquisition, but Spanish and English certainly share more cognates than Russian and English. This similarity may be enough to help beginning learners begin to process meaning sooner in Spanish than in Russian—and processing meaning in the input is a prerequisite for acquisition.

Pause to consider . . .

how the alphabet system might affect acquisition. How is being literate helpful in learning an L2? What happens when the alphabets don't resemble each other? Do you think that differences in alphabet have an effect if the languages are acquired in a *completely oral context*? For example, in day-to-day situations, do you think an English speaker would have more difficulty learning Russian or Japanese than Italian?

WHAT MAKES SOME STRUCTURES DIFFICULT AND SOME EASY TO ACQUIRE?

Several decades ago, the answer to the question, When is a structure difficult to acquire? would have been, Whenever the L1 rule and L2 rule are different. Teachers are quick to say, for example, that the subjunctive in Romance languages is difficult because it doesn't exist in English (although there is some subjunctive verb use left in English, e.g., *I really prefer that he not go;* the regular present tense for *he* would be *goes*). Or they might say that the case system in Russian is difficult because English doesn't have case (even though pronouns do have case, e.g., *he* vs. *him*). But as we have seen, SLA consists of different processes with different factors influencing each process. At the same time, the processes don't all act on the same data; some act on input, some act on processed input, some act on data already in the system, some make use of explicit knowledge, and so on. We also know that a transfer-based explanation for difficulty is dicey because of the difficulty in researching transfer; we don't know how it works.

The best explanation for what makes a rule difficult is that different aspects of acquisition come together to make it difficult. Let's take the subjunctive in Romance languages, for example. In input processing, the subjunctive is an item of low communicative value and will tend not to get processed; any meaning it carries is already indicated by the main clause (e.g., doubt, denial), at least in cases of noun clauses. In addition, the present subjunctive is not nearly as frequent in the input as other verb forms. The present indicative tends to dominate, followed by the simple past, and so on, with the present subjunctive coming in last. In one count, the subjunctive made up only 5 percent of the verbs used. At the same time, the subjunctive requires that all of the output procedures discussed in Chapter 4 be acquired, since the learner has to carry grammatical information across a clause boundary (the most difficult procedure in the hierarchy). And, if we accepted a transfer-based explanation in acquisition, the structure exists only in remnants in English. The subjunctive, then, has a quadruple whammy going against it.

There may not be a simple explanation, then, for the difficulty associated with acquiring some rules and structures. Instead, we should look to multiple factors that coalesce to explain the difficulty. We must also take into consideration, however, whether the question is about acquisition or about classroom rule learning. For explicit teaching and learning, the subjunctive may indeed be difficult because there is little of it in English. As learners work through explanations and rules and try to keep them in their head, they can't rely on English to help out. But classroom rule learning is not the same as acquisition. Acquisition is, to emphasize the point, multifaceted.

Pause to consider . . .

aspects of language that may be easy to learn explicitly but difficult to produce. English third-person *–s* is an easy rule to learn explicitly, but according to research, it is one of the inflections that learners have the most difficulty with in spoken speech. Placement of object pronouns in Spanish is not a difficult rule to learn explicitly, but learners consistently miscomprehend object-verb-subject word order. Knowing what you know, how can you account for these observations?

DOESN'T EVERYTHING IN SLA COME DOWN TO MOTIVATION?

As teachers, we often lament students' lack of motivation in language learning, especially in foreign language classrooms in the United States. As a language program director, I even hear such statements from students as, "I hate this stupid language requirement"; lack of motivation couldn't be clearer than that. Motivation is a big component of all our endeavors in everyday life. If we need to diet, we have to be motivated. If we need to go to the gym, we have to be motivated. And my doctoral students tell me they go through periods when they are not motivated to work on their dissertations.

But note that motivation relates only to whether or not we do something and how far we get. A really motivated person may lose 20 pounds on a diet while a less motivated person may lose only 10. A really motivated doctoral student may write the dissertation in one month while another takes years. Motivation, however, does not tell us anything about how the task is done. What are the processes involved? What does the activity the person is engaged in look like? What are the steps along the way?

In SLA, motivation works the same way; it can be a good predictor of how far people get in language acquisition. There has even been research on two different kinds of motivation: integrative motivation and instrumental motivation. The former refers to the desire to be part of the L2 group (you want to "integrate"); the latter refers to the desire to use the L2 for practical purposes (it is an "instrument" to achieve a professional goal, for example). In general, people with high degrees of motivation learn more language than those with less motivation. Research has also shown, however, that motivation can result from success in the L2; if the learning is enjoyable and learners see the fruits of their endeavors, they become motivated to learn more. This is called resultative motivation.

Again, as in other contexts, motivation does not tell us anything about how acquisition happens, and it can't explain the phenomena that we see. For example, motivation cannot explain the universality of acquisition orders and developmental stages. It cannot explain the difficulty or ease learners experience in acquiring particular rules. It cannot explain accented speech. So, although important for eventual success, motivation lacks the power to help us understand the processes involved in acquisition.

Pause to consider . . .

your own motivation in learning another language (assuming that you have). What was your motivation? How far do you think you've gotten in mastering the language? Are you happy with where you are or would you like to progress? Can you cite things you have done (to acquire language) that are a result of your motivation?

DOES AGE MAKE A DIFFERENCE IN LANGUAGE LEARNING?

Children are remarkable creatures. How they change from babies to toddlers and then to school-age kids is amazing, whether you chart their physical growth, their cognitive-intellectual development, or their language acquisition. They seem to be sponges when it comes to life, soaking everything up and learning at very quick rates. They also seem to have the upper hand when it comes to SLA. It is common to hear people remark on how easily children pick up another language or say that if you really want to learn another language, you should start while you're a child. And to a large extent this is true, but not always for the reason that many think it is so.

One construct that has been posited in the SLA literature is the *critical period,* as mentioned in Chapter 1. According to some scholars, people pass through a critical period after which it is almost impossible to acquire another language. The critical period is said to end in late childhood or puberty. If you don't start learning a second language before then, you're in trouble (or at least you can't learn a language like a child does). Aside from everyday experience, the critical period has found some support in SLA research. Some studies have compared L2 learners who began learning before puberty and those who began learning after (that is, they arrived in the United States before puberty or after). The researchers have administered speaking tests, grammaticality judgments, and other measures to see just how native-like the learners become. The research strongly suggests that those who fall on the prepuberty side tend to perform much better than those who do not, and in many cases are indistinguishable from native speakers.

But, as you might suspect, the issue is not so clear-cut. Other scholars have reexamined the research and have pointed out that if you remove the critical period and simply look at the age of onset of learning (when the person began the task of acquisition) and performance on all the tests, you get a fairly good correlation. Put another way, the earlier you start, the better; starting at 40 is better than starting at 60, 20 is better than 40, and 10 is better than 20. There is no magical cut-off point. This correlation suggests that acquisition boils down to time on task. The younger you start, the more time you have to spend on acquisition. If you start at 10 and get tested when you're 40, you've spent 30 years acquiring language. If you start at 20 and get tested when you're 40, you've spent one-third less time! In addition, children engage in interactions with other speakers and in particular kinds of interactions that adults do not. Adults may have L2 interactions on the job or in the marketplace while speaking the L1 with the spouse and perhaps close friends, especially in so-called ethnic communities, but children go to school and study, play, take up sports, get into trouble, and engage in all kinds of socializing activities with the L2 as the medium of communication. Their acquisition is more "round the clock" and their communicative contexts are much more varied than is true for adults.

Other research has found that adolescents are best at initial startup. They get further than adults or children in the beginning stages, and they get there faster. Adults are better at initial startup than children. However, like the research above, this research also shows that in the long run, children are better learners; they get further and acquire more in the end.

So, in spite of the fact that children are amazing little beings, it is not clear that they are truly special when it comes to SLA; it may be that the environmental and social cards are simply stacked in their favor. Like children learning a first language, child L2 learners engage in activities and behaviors that are absolutely conducive to acquisition; adolescents and adults do not. It is still possible that the mechanisms for language acquisition don't work as well for adolescents and adults as they do for children, but it is clear that the mechanisms don't shut off completely.

With that said, it is important to distinguish between the acquisition of the sound system and the acquisition of everything else. The research clearly shows that the sound system is much more resistant to native-like pronunciation than, say, syntax (sentence structure). In some studies, learners have been shown to develop higher levels of syntactic knowledge and ability than phonological knowledge and ability in the long run. That is, their syntactic components seem to be more likely to approach native-like status than their phonological components. To be sure, some research has shown that some learners do attain phonological abilities (and knowledge) in the L2 that are indistinguishable from those of natives. However, the majority of studies on the age factor have not focused on the sound system because of the belief that it is more resistant. (There is also a bias in language studies in general toward sentence structure, so that linguists who research phonology are in the minority to begin with.)

Pause to consider . . .

how much actual time an adult might spend in the acquisition of a language. How many hours a day would that person spend interacting in commu-nicative contexts using the language? Does living in a place where the lan-guage is spoken assure constant con-tact with speakers? Why or why not?

DON'T DIFFERENT LEVELS OF LEARNERS NEED DIFFERENT THINGS TO HELP THEM KEEP LEARNING?

In many language programs around the world, beginning students get one kind of course, intermediate students another, and the more advanced take courses in literature, linguistics, or some other content area related to the lan-guage. These differences are dictated by institutional concerns (e.g., in the United States, beginning language courses may be a general education require-ment whereas the more advanced courses are designed for students with a major or minor in a language). These differences are not dictated by what we know about SLA, but they may inadvertently help.

For acquisition, beginners need input that is manageable. It cannot be the same kind of language that native speakers use with each other. It cannot be a steady diet of native-speaking television, either. As beginners progress, they need access to more and more complex input, so that the internal processes can continue to map new forms and structures onto meaning. And for maximum vocabulary development, learners need to read all along the way, since most vocabulary development in both L1 and L2 acquisition is incidental, meaning that vocabulary is learned as a by-product of some other intention (normally reading).

Learners also need interaction all along the way. We have seen how inter-action can help learners capture things they have missed before. And they need interaction because speaking skills and output procedures need to be acquired and developed. For beginners, output demands should be minimal, although some contexts will always require them to push themselves beyond their cur-rent limits. (My grandmother, who spoke only minimal English, would often take one of us grandchildren with her when she needed to conduct business so that communication breakdowns would be minimized.)

Most aspects of what learners need happen naturally as they progress. As native speakers perceive that learners have more or less control over the lan-guage, they adjust their speech up or down. This adjustment makes the input more or less appropriate. Native speakers often adjust the interaction as well, so that if they perceive learners to have minimal or little control over the language, they place fewer output demands on them. For example, a doctor may switch from "Where does it hurt?" to "Does it hurt here? Does it hurt here?" because yes/no questions demand less output than open-ended questions. The reason adjustments happen is that acquisition occurs in some kind of communicative context. As long as people are trying to communicate, they do what they need to do to make communication happen. (In the Epilogue, we include some suggestions about teaching language in classrooms at different levels.)

95

What about Individual Differences? Should I Consider Learning Styles?

Pause to consider . . .

what you have just read. Which of the following would thus make the most sense to you? (1) Learners always need the same things no matter where they are in terms of development. They just need different quantities of the ingredients. (2) Learners always need the same things no matter where they are in terms of development. The difference is in the quality of the ingredients.

WHAT ABOUT INDIVIDUAL DIFFERENCES? SHOULD I CONSIDER LEARNING STYLES?

Human beings differ in how they approach tasks (if not life). On a gross level, some people are more visual than others. Some are more cerebral than others. When it comes to how people handle information, various tests have been developed that tell people to what extent they are, for example, concrete or abstract, random or sequential. It goes without saying, then, that **individual differences** in learning affect how people gather, assimilate, and make use of information in everyday life. I may take more notes than you or make visual representations of things. You may prefer to discuss and review with someone else. You may tolerate ambiguity and not need clarification right away, whereas I might not be able to wait for the ambiguity to clear up and might have to interrupt to say, "I'm sorry. I don't get it." What about individual differences in SLA?

A fundamental assumption of this book has been that SLA is different from other kinds of learning because language processors are designed to work only on language. At the same time, language acquisition needs the language processors or the brain won't get the data and shape them the way it needs to. The question then becomes, How do individual differences in nonlanguage learning affect SLA, if at all? In language teaching, the 1990s were witness to increased work on learning styles and their match or mismatch with teaching styles. However, no research has yet found a link between learning styles and individual differences, on the one hand, and the processes involved in language acquisition on the other. The issue of individual differences may be important when it comes to the creation of explicit knowledge or the presentation of explicit information, but as we have seen, explicit knowledge and the processes that use it operate independently of the processors that work on language. Explicit knowledge and its use are subject to the same kinds of learning issues as any kind of information learning. (It is worth pointing out that no one has researched the matter of individual differences and nonclassroom learning; the research has been exclusively on classroom learners and mostly on foreign language learners.) So what does a learning difference, such as linear thinking versus nonlinear thinking, have to do with how the brain builds the network of lexical items or how restructuring happens in the syntactic component of the developing system? What does the difference between being more or less visual have to do with the acquisition of output-processing procedures? The answer is that there are no direct connections. Before we explore whether there might be indirect connections, let's return to basics.

Language acquisition happens in only one way and all learners must undergo it. Learners must have exposure to communicative input and they must process it; the brain must organize data. Learners must acquire output procedures, and they need to interact with other speakers. There is no way around these fundamental aspects of acquisition; they are the basics. The types of individual differences that may directly affect acquisition are those involved in *working memory.* In at least one model of working memory, research has been done on different capacities for processing and storing information during the act of comprehension. Although everyone has a **limited capacity** in working memory, the research suggests that some people's working memories are more limited than others. There are even tests that examine individual differences in working memory in L1 reading and listening comprehension. Since input processing takes place in working memory, could it be that learners vary in their capacities to process incoming information? If so, then these differences should show up in comprehension; and if they show up in comprehension, they should show up in acquisition. (Remember, for input to be of use, it must be communicative and learners must be actively engaged in trying to comprehend the message.)

This scenario does not mean that people go through different acquisition orders or stages because of differences in working memory. It means that some people have more room in working memory and may acquire language faster than others. Some, with very limited working memory, may have so much trouble with comprehension that they become frustrated and tune out the input. (There may differences in capacity for output processing as well. The procedures required for speech production take place in real time and there is a working memory for production as well. For example, with the subordinate clause procedure, a speaker must hold grammatical information in working memory until that part of the clause is produced where that information can be applied. However, individual differences on the output end of things have not been researched in either L1 or L2.) But note that even these individual differences in working memory do not affect the processes or procedures themselves; they affect how much of the process or procedure can be used at a given point in time.

Let's return to the other kind of individual differences, differences in learning style (as opposed to differences in working memory). One possibility that research has yet to examine is that learning styles may interact with how learners handle input. To offer just one example, let's say that person A's learning style is random, meaning that his thinking and processing of information do not require a step-by-step presentation with follow-through. Person B's learning style is sequential, meaning that information and tasks have to flow in a certain way for her to learn. She dislikes tangents and extraneous information that get in the way of the task. Person A may not have any problem with free-flowing input and may be willing to jump right into a conversation, let's say. Person B, however, may prefer a more structured situation or one that can be controlled. Person B may like to work through individual sentences and be sure she understands before going on. Person A may tolerate ambiguity more and allow comprehension to "develop." In this one scenario, we see that although both learners ultimately need input for acquisition, they might benefit from different kinds of input, especially in the beginning phases of acquisition.

In short, learning styles and individual differences need to be linked to what we know about acquisition for them to be of use to us. They could be linked to input, input management, type of input, quality of the input, and so on. This is where the research on learning differences needs to head if it is to help language teachers link the concepts of individual differences with what they understand about SLA.

Pause to consider . . .

why learning styles might be important in an academic context for language learning rather than in a nonclassroom immersion context.

WHAT'S THE BEST METHOD FOR TEACHING AND LEARNING?

Teachers are concerned with methodology (the "how to" of teaching), and rightly so. At language teaching conferences, I am often asked, What's the best teaching method? Teachers want to know the "right way" or the "best way" to do things. Part of this concern comes from the history of language teaching, in which methods have paraded across academic institutions like balloons in the Thanksgiving Day parade. Here's a partial list of methods that we have seen in just the last seventy years:

- Grammar-Translation
- the Silent Way
- Audiolingual Method
- Counseling Language Learning
- the Natural Approach
- Total Physical Response
- Strategic Interaction
- the Berlitz Method
- Suggestopedia
- Cognitive-Code

For many, it seems if you don't jump on a method bandwagon, you'll be left behind. And indeed, many language education curricula and graduate teaching assistant programs have a course that usually contains the word "methods" or "methodology" in it. But with such a plethora of methods, how do you choose? How do you know what's right? Some claim to have an eclectic method, eschewing any allegiance to a particular method and grabbing pieces from various methods that suit their daily and curricular needs.

When asked the question about the right method, I invariably respond that there is none. I explain that in applied SLA circles (that is, language teaching theory and research), few adhere to the concept of "methods." Instead, we talk about *principled approaches* to language instruction. By *principled approaches* we mean instructional efforts that are based on principles derived from knowledge about language and communication, about second language acquisition and second language use, and about affective responses in humans. In short, teachers can't grab from here and there to suit their immediate needs; they can grab from here and there if what they grab reflects one of the principles underlying their approach. Eclecticism is fine as long as it is informed and guided by something other than distaste for methods in general.

I also hear people say that they use "the communicative method" when teaching. This is an odd term, since there is no single communicative method. There are various communicative approaches, each informed by its own principles, and many of which overlap. For example, in contemporary language teaching, the following are all communicative approaches: the Natural Approach, task-based learning, immersion, and content-based instruction (discussed in more detail in the Epilogue). What makes them all communicative is that they share the principle that *communication is at the heart of language acquisition*, that is, that people acquire language by engaging in communicative behaviors, which are the interpretation, expression, and negotiation of meaning. Each communicative approach involves these three aspects of communication to a greater or lesser degree because of the particular materials they use and the contexts in which learning occurs.

SUMMARY

In this chapter we asked and answered a good number of frequently asked questions on topics ranging from the role of the first language (transfer) in SLA to the role of drills in teaching and learning to the role of instruction in general. We also addressed questions that were concerned with differences and similarities between first and second language acquisition and with individual differences and learning styles. In short, we touched upon a number of issues that were not addressed in previous chapters but could be answered only after we had a foundation with which to answer them. When we reviewed the givens of SLA in Chapter 1 and then the various processes and products in subsequent chapters, we laid the groundwork that would allow us to adequately address the types of questions that teachers and others often have about both SLA and language teaching.

Two points have emerged from answering these questions. The first concerns beliefs. A good number of the questions stem from teachers' beliefs about how languages are acquired. These beliefs are not confined to a small set of instructors but are typical of what I hear from people who do not have a background in current SLA research and theory. The point is this: The answers to the questions go against many of the beliefs that teachers hold (and indeed against the beliefs of many who are not teachers). Perhaps it is time, as a profession, to use what we know about SLA to examine such beliefs.

The second point that emerged is that the effects of certain kinds of instructional efforts are limited and in some cases are nil. In Spanish we have a saying: *mucho ruido y pocas nueces* (lots of noise but few nuts—referring to squirrels rustling in the leaves on the ground but coming up empty-handed.) This saying suggests that a lot of effort may go into doing something, with very little effect. Much of what teachers do in a direct attempt to induce grammar and language in learners' heads may be questionable. Much of what textbook authors provide as ways of "practicing" grammar is fruitless. By addressing certain questions that teachers often ask, we have shown that the learner, ultimately, is the one in charge of acquisition. We can only provide opportunities for acquisition to happen (if that is our intent). In the Epilogue, we examine some implications of SLA research that can serve as the outline for creating such opportunities.

READ MORE ABOUT IT

L1 Transfer

Gass, S. M., & Selinker, L. (1992). *Language transfer in language learning.* Philadelphia: Benjamins. ▲

White, L. (2000). Second language acquisition: From initial to final state. In J. Archibald (Ed.), *Second language acquisition and linguistic theory.* Oxford: Blackwell. ▲

L1 in the L2 Classroom

Brooks, F., Donato, R., & McGlone, J. V. (1997). When are they going to say 'it' right? Understanding learner talk during pair-work activity. *Foreign Language Annals, 30*, 525–541.

L1 Acquisition and SLA Compared

A good deal of empirical research conducted since the 1970s makes overt comparisons between L1 and L2 acquisition, using various frameworks. A good place to begin is the following:

Hatch, E. M. (1978). *Second language acquisition: A book of readings.* Rowley, MA: Newbury House. [See especially "Is second language learning like the first?" by S. Ervin-Tripp (1974), reprinted from *TESOL Quarterly, 8*, 111–127.]

Another book that makes explicit comparisons between L1 and L2 in terms of the basic problems in the acquisition of syntax is the following:

White, L. (1989). *Universal grammar and second language acquisition.* Philadelphia: Benjamins. ▲

A variety of more current readings dealing with syntax also make comparisons, although they can be quite challenging for the novice, for example:

Lardiere, D. (2000). Mapping features to forms in second language acquisition. In J. Archibald (Ed.), *Second language acquisition and linguistic theory*, (pp. 102–129). Oxford: Blackwell. ▲

Imitation and Repetition

There is no single place to direct you to for reading about imitation and repetition in SLA. If you begin to read more in SLA, you will undoubtedly uncover the arguments against their role as major causative factors in acquisition. You may wish to read something in child L1 acquisition in which imitation and repetition are empirically falsified as major factors, such as:

Brown, R. (1973). *A first language: The early stages.* Cambridge, MA: Harvard University Press.

The Effect of Drills

Lightbown, P. (1983). Exploring relationships between developmental and instructional sequences in L2 acquisition. In H. W. Seliger & M. H. Long (Eds.), *Classroom oriented research in second language acquisition* (pp. 217–243). Rowley, MA: Newbury House.

VanPatten, B. (2002). Processing instruction: An update. *Language Learning, 52,* 755–803.

Explicit Rules

Schmidt, R. (Ed.). (1995). *Attention and awareness in foreign language learning.* Honolulu: University of Hawaii Second Language Teaching and Curriculum Center. [Not all contributions in the volume are relevant to this topic, but they are all relevant to various topics discussed in this book.]

VanPatten, B., & Oikennon, S. (1996). Explanation versus structured input in processing instruction. *Studies in Second Language Acquisition, 18,* 495–510. [See also VanPatten, B. (2002) under The Effect of Drills for other studies similar to VanPatten and Oikennon.]

Schwartz, B. (1993). On explicit and negative data effecting and affecting competence and linguistic behavior. *Studies in Second Language Acquisition, 15,* 147–164.

Error Correction and Recasts

Mackey, A., & Philip, J. (1999). Conversational interaction and second language development: Recasts, responses and red herrings. *The Modern Language Journal, 82,* 338–356.

Ortega, L., & Long, M. H. (1997). The effects of models and recasts on the acquisition of object topicalization and adverb placement in L2 Spanish. *Spanish Applied Linguistics, 1,* 65–86.

See also Schwartz (1993) under Explicit Rules. Negative data is a term that encompasses error correction.

The Effects of Instruction

A tremendous amount of literature exists in this area. Here are some sample places to begin reading.

Doughty, C., & Williams, J. (Eds.) (1998). *Focus on form*. Cambridge: Cambridge University Press.

Lightbown, P., Spada, N., & White, L. (1993). The role of instruction in second language acquisition. Special issue of *Studies in Second Language Acquisition*, June. ▲

Long, M. H. (1983). Does second language instruction make a difference? A review of the research. *TESOL Quarterly, 17*, 359–382.

Norris, J. M., & Ortega, L. (2000). Effectiveness of L2 instruction: A research synthesis and quantitative meta-analysis. *Language Learning, 50*, 417–528. ▲

Motivation

Crookes, G., & Schmidt, R. (1991). Motivation: Reopening the research agenda. *Language Learning, 31*, 469–512.

Gardner, R. (1985). *Social psychology and second language learning: The role of attitude and motivation*. London: Edward Arnold.

Age

Bialystok, E., & Hakuta, K. (1994). *In other words*. New York: Basic Books. [See Chapter 3, Brain.]

Birdsong, D. (1999). *Second language acquisition and the critical period hypothesis*. Mahwah, NJ: Erlbaum. [See especially Chapter 1, Why's and Why Nots of the Critical Period Hypothesis for Second Language Acquisition.] ▲

Johnson, J. S., & Newport, E. (1989). Critical period effects in second language learning: The influence of maturational state on the acquisition of English as a second language. *Cognitive Psychology, 21*, 60–99.

Krashen, S. D., Scarcella, R. C., & Long, M. H. (Eds.). (1982). *Child–adult differences in second language acquisition*. Rowley, MA: Newbury House. [See especially the last three chapters.]

Individual Differences and Learning Styles

Just, M. A., & Carpenter, P. A. (1993). A capacity theory of comprehension: Individual differences in working memory. *Psychological Review, 99*, 122–149. ▲

Oxford, R. (1990). *Language learning strategies: What every teacher should know*. Rowley, MA: Newbury House.

Skehan, P. (1989). *Individual differences in second language learning*. London: Edward Arnold.

Methods

Bardovi-Harlig, K., & Hartford, B. (Eds.). (1997). *Beyond methods: Components of second language teacher education*. New York: McGraw-Hill.

Richards, J., & Rodgers, R. (1986). *Approaches and methods in language teaching*. Cambridge: Cambridge University Press.

Epilogue: Implications for Teaching

Until now, the focus of this book has been largely on SLA and not teaching. You have been introduced to some basic concepts and research findings in SLA (with caveats noted where appropriate), and if you had any preconceived notions about how SLA happens, either they were confirmed or you had the rug yanked out from under you.

In this chapter, we end the book with some general implications for language teaching that is acquisition-oriented. The point is not to exhaust the possibilities of approaches or techniques or to provide lots of samples for what to do Monday in class. Rather, the idea here is to be suggestive and to stimulate thinking and provide references for further reading. You may already do some of these things in class. If so, perhaps you have found justification in this book for your own intuitions. None of these implications is necessarily new; they may simply be new to readers who have not heard of them before.

One other thing to keep in mind is that language teaching does not have to be acquisition-oriented. If a curriculum designer believes that the purpose of language study in an academic setting is to learn grammar and vocabulary for reading the "great works" or to improve the intellectual and analytical abilities of students, that director has the right to use a non-acquisition-oriented curriculum. In short, the acquisition of language may not be every curriculum's goal. But if it is your goal, perhaps the suggestions here will stimulate thinking in the appropriate directions.

IMPLICATION 1: THE MORE INPUT, THE BETTER (THE MORE MEANING-BASED THE CLASS, THE BETTER)

A recurring theme in this book has been the fundamental or critical role that input plays in acquisition. Remember that input is defined as language the learner hears or reads that has communicative intent or is meaning-based; the learner's job is to get the message contained in that language. Language teaching curricula that incorporate input as much as possible are curricula that encourage language acquisition. At the same time, the more curricula strive to put communication at the center of lessons, which means that meaning becomes central rather than form alone, the more those curricula are likely to provide optimal input.

Input can be incorporated into a language-teaching curriculum in many ways. *Immersion* and *content-based instruction* are two. In these kinds of curricula, learners don't actually focus on language itself; rather, they learn some kind of subject matter or other content *through* the second language. A math class, a science lab, a course on geography, a cooking school, even drivers' education and training sessions if done in the second language are all examples of immersion or content-based instruction. Another kind of instruction in which input plays a major role is the **Natural Approach.** Developed by Tracy Terrell, this approach brings together a number of techniques and practices that use input to encourage acquisition: total physical response, particular kinds of vocabulary presentations, picture-files and their use in making meaning understood, and others.

Other approaches have emerged that are hybrids and derivatives of content-based instruction or the Natural Approach, all of which include lots of input in and out of the classroom. And of course, reading level-appropriate (comprehensible) material that is of interest to learners is always an excellent way to supplement teaching with written input.

Many teachers have been presenting vocabulary via input for years. Most standard texts have thematic vocabulary groupings: family, food and drink, traveling, clothing, and so on. Once you get the hang of it, it is quite easy to take these lists and fashion a presentation all in the L2. The trick is to keep some informational goal (meaning) in sight so that you don't slide into a mere presentation of the vocabulary. In the example below, the instructor's goal is not just "to teach family vocabulary" but also to have students be able to match names to the relationships within his family. (The original teacher input was in Spanish.)

Today we are going to talk about my family. I have a most interesting family. (*Displays "My Family" chart on board or overhead.*) Here is me. These are my parents. This is my father and this is my mother. Father . . . mother. My father's name is Bill. My mother's name is Juanita. They are divorced. This is my stepfather, Joe. My stepfather. And this is my sister . . . my only sister. Her name is Gloria. (*Turns off the overhead or covers visual.*)

Let's see what kind of memory you have. What is my father's name—Joe or Bill? (*responses*) What is my mother's name—Juanita or Gloria? (*responses*) Right. Gloria is my sister, not my mother. And do I have any brothers? (*responses*) No. (*Shows visual again.*) All right, to summarize, my family consists of my father, Bill, my mother, Juanita, and my sister, Gloria. I have no brothers. Oh, I also have a stepfather, Joe. My parents have been divorced since 1972. (*Writes date on board.*) Now, that was easy, but here are some other family members. (*Now reveals grandparents.*)

These are my grandparents. My grandparents. These are my maternal grandparents and these are my paternal grandparents. This man here, Dick, is my paternal grandfather. And this woman, Bridgette, is my paternal grandmother. Grandfather . . . grandmother. But Bridgette passed away many years ago; Bridgette is dead. (*Points to tombstone.*) These are my maternal grandparents. Domingo is my paternal grandfather . . . and Concepción is my maternal grandmother. Domingo passed away in 1985; Domingo is dead. Just to review, Dick and Bridgette are my paternal grandparents, and Domingo and Concepción are my maternal grandparents. Grandfather . . . grandfather . . . grandmother . . . grandmother. Both Bridgette and Domingo are dead. By the way, Dick lives in Indiana and Concepción lives in California. (*Removes or covers visual.*)

   Ready for a real memory test? (*Shows new overhead, or distributes ditto.*) In the left column are names; in the right column are relationships. You have two minutes to match the name to a relationship. (*After two minutes, teacher calls time and quiz is reviewed with original drawing exposed; teacher engages in some light conversation in which students answer with one-word, "yes/no" responses, such as, "Did you know that I was half Mexican? How does your family compare to mine—do you have more brothers and sisters?"*)

   Now, here is the real interesting part. (*Reveals visual of extended family with aunts and uncles, some cousins, and so on. Instructor continues presentation using same format as before.*) (Lee & VanPatten, 1995, pp. 46–47)

   In presenting food, the meaning goal might be cataloging likes and dislikes or learning a recipe. With travel-related vocabulary, the meaning goal might be to match certain personality types with traveling style. Input without a meaning goal, without communicative intent, can slip into just more language practice. If learners perceive that they don't have to pay attention, they won't. (Note how in the example above, the instructor quizzes repeatedly on the information conveyed.)

IMPLICATION 2: THE MORE INTERACTION, THE BETTER

For a number of years, "communicative interchanges" in classrooms were (and maybe still are) dominated by a particular approach: The teacher asks questions and the students answer—and almost always these interactions have had a hidden grammatical agenda. Teachers asked questions so that students would then use a particular grammatical structure in their answers. This practice has led to some rather unnatural if not bizarre patterns of interaction that do not look at all like the kind that facilitate acquisition as we have discussed in this book. An example of an instructor who insists on teaching while "talking" with her students is given below. Note how the communication and thus interaction degenerates into silence on the part of the students as they realize that the point is not really to converse. (The original dialogue was in French.)

TEACHER: Do you think there is really one French personality, a typically French personality?
Yes?

STUDENTS: No.

TEACHER: No? Why?
  (Pause)
  Claudia?
STUDENT: Um . . . I think that there's a . . .
TEACHER: *(Interrupting)* That there's a French personality?
  Good. Describe the French personality.
STUDENT: How do you say "pride"?
TEACHER: Oh . . . You've already had two words.
  (Writing on blackboard) Okay, "la fierté" is like in English
  "pride," and the adjective, "fier."
  Je suis fier, I'm proud.
  Good, are the French very proud?
  Do they have a lot of pride?
  (Silence)
  Are the French nationalistic?

(Lee & VanPatten, 1995, p. 9)

Contrast the preceding teacher–student interaction with the following one. In this example, notice how the students are participating actively (and notice the kind of language they use and how the interaction allows them to produce level-appropriate output).

Phase 1: Associations

  I: I am going to tell you a word and I want to know everything that you associate with this word. Ready? The word is "bilingual." What do you associate with "bilingual"?
  S1: Two languages.
  I: Two languages. Two languages. What else?
  S2: English/Spanish.
  I: English/Spanish. Uh huh. Especially in the dictionary, the bilingual dictionary you have. What else?
  S1: Education.
  I: Education. There is this phenomenon of bilingual education in this country. Very good. What else? Do you associate the term with certain people, for example, or not?
  S3: Yes.
  I: Yes? For example, anyone in particular?
  S3: Persons is their parents a-a-are from another country. Fir-first generation here.
  I: Yes. The first generation of a family often is bilingual. The second and third, sometimes not. Then if the parents are from other countries, bilingualism is also associated with immigration. The family, immigration, education, two languages, what else? English/Spanish. What else?
  S4: A morning class.
  I: A morning class but at a very convenient hour. Yes. I have another term for you. Another idea and I want to know what you associate with this word. It is "bicultural." Not bilingual, but bicultural. What do you associate with that term, with "bicultural"?
  S1: Two countries.

I: Two countries. Uh hmm. What else?

S1: A life in your house and [*Inaudible.*]

I: Differences?

S1: Yes.

I: The home culture and the out-of-the-home culture. What else? [*5-second pause.*] Do you associate food with biculturalism?

SS: [*General murmuring.*]

I: Yes? Other things?

S3: Someone they have parents from two countries, different ones.

I: Oh. For example, one parent is from the United States and the other is from Mexico, for example. The parents represent two different cultures. Okay.

Phase 2: Becoming bilingual/bicultural

I: Umm, now. I have something else for you. How can you, in the future, how can you become bilinguals? How can you become bilingual? What can you do to be, to become bilingual? What are some ideas? What can you propose to me?

S1: Bilingual was very important for communication.

I: Yes. Bilingualism is important for communication. Uh huh. But how can you, what can you do to be bilingual? What can you do to become bilingual?

S3: Take a lot of Spanish.

I: Ah, very good. Very good answer. Take classes. Take classes. This is one way to become bilingual. Formally study the language. Other ways that do not have to do with school?

S5: You go to the, to the country of the language.

I: To me the idea seems very good. Go to where this language is spoken. It is a very good idea. A very good way. Other ways? [*5-second pause.*] I imagine that it is a little expensive to go to live in another country but . . . What else can you do?

S1: Talk with people of other languages.

I: Talk to bilingual people. There are a lot of bilinguals here in Champaign/Urbana. You can have contact with these people. Something else? [*4-second pause.*] Now I have another question, perhaps a little more difficult. Okay. How can you become bicultural? One thing is to know two languages, another thing is to be bicultural. What ideas can you propose to me? How can you become bicultural? [*9-second pause.*]

S1: I do not understand the question.

I: Okay. We have three ideas about becoming bilingual. Go to a country, study the language, another one that I do not remember. Now I want to know what can you do to be bicultural people? To be a person with two cultures. [*5-second pause.*]

Phase 3: Conclusion

I: I have one more question. Do you believe, and I want to see hands, do you believe that a person can be bilingual without being bicultural? That is, a person can speak two languages but the person does not have two cultures. How many believe it is true? [*Raise hands.*] Many, many. Why do you believe this?

S5: A person studies the language in his own country and not go to another country.

  I: That's it. If someone studies the language without having contact with the culture. It seems to me that the person could be bilingual without being bicultural. Uh huh. Other reasons?

S3: Someone can learn only the language in his school, school, and not have so-someone culture than the language.

  I: If you do not have contact with people who represent the culture and if you only have contact in school, yes, this can be the result. Yes?

S2: My mother is bilingual and was in two culturals but she does not practice two culturals.

  I: Your mother is bilingual? And you say she is bicultural or not?

S2: She does not practice two but knows two.

  I: She does not practice the two cultures. What are the two cultures?

S2: Spanish and *Japanese.*

  I: Japanese. The Spanish culture and the Japanese culture.

S2: And very different.

  I: They are two different cultures, very different. Anything else?

(Lee, 2000, pp. 62–64)

Classrooms in which interactions truly focus on meaning and are level-appropriate for learners will foster acquisition. Such interactions can be found in task-oriented activities in which the task has a particular communicative or informational goal. The task, of course, must be appropriate for beginning, intermediate, or advanced learners. Tasks for beginners may require minimum output or output that is easily produced based on a model; to put this a different way, the task may be heavily structured with lots of linguistic support built in. Tasks for more advanced learners could be less structured. Here is an example of a task for beginners that promotes interaction.

Activity. What Did You Do Last Week?

Step 1. Working with a partner, indicate if each activity is physically sedentary or active. You and your partner must agree on the categorization.

	SEDENTARY	ACTIVE
1. dancing at a party	❑	❑
2. riding a bike	❑	❑
3. playing video games	❑	❑
4. playing a sport	❑	❑
5. reading a book	❑	❑
6. watching TV	❑	❑
7. writing a letter	❑	❑
8. making dinner	❑	❑

Does the rest of the class agree with your categorizations of these activities?

Step 2. Add three activities to the list, preferably three that you or your partner engage in, and indicate whether or not they are sedentary.

	SEDENTARY	ACTIVE
_____	❑	❑
_____	❑	❑
_____	❑	❑

Compare your activities with those of your classmates. Do you all
engage in similar activities?

Step 3. Interview your partner about what he or she did last week. Keep track
of the answers because you will need them in Step 4.

MODEL: —Did you play any sports last week?
—I played tennis twice last week.

Step 4. Compare your partner's responses to the categorizations you made in
Steps 1 and 2. Then use the following scale to rate your partner's week.

VERY SEDENTARY		AS SEDENTARY AS ACTIVE		VERY ACTIVE
1	2	3	4	5

Step 5. Using your evaluations of each other's level of activity, draw a class
profile. Overall, to what degree was everyone's week sedentary or
active?

(Lee, 2000, p. 37)

Again, the point here is that interaction promotes acquisition because students help to manage the input. During the interaction, the input may be modified by the other speaker to maximize communication. Certain aspects of the
input may then become more salient to learners during the course of that modification. Interaction may also heighten learners' awareness of things that are
missing in their developing systems, pushing them to be more active input
processors.

IMPLICATION 3: ALL LEARNER PRODUCTION
SHOULD BE MEANING-BASED, OR
COMMUNICATIVE

This implication is actually a follow-up to the previous one. What it suggests is
that *whenever* learners produce language, it should be for the purpose of
expressing some kind of meaning. As we saw in Chapter 5, the usefulness of

mechanical drills for promoting either acquisition or productive abilities is questionable. Thus, learners should not spend their time producing utterances for the sake of producing utterances. At the same time, learners should not be forced to produce if they are not ready nor should it be expected that their production be free and unconstrained. Simply stated, when production is required, it should be communicative in nature.

Learners can produce meaningful sentences not only in interactive tasks like those described earlier but also in tasks with a grammatical focus. In one technique, called **structured output,** learners use one form throughout the task to create meaning. Here's an example. It is translated from Spanish and the focus is on the reciprocal reflexive to express actions done to one another.

Step 1. Indicate if each action is typical or not in your family. You may add another item if you wish.

1. We hug each other when we see each other.

2. We kiss each other when we see each other.

3. We greet each other in the morning.

4. We call each other on the phone a lot.

5. We support each other.

6. We understand each other well.

7. _____

Step 2. Using the ideas from Step 1, create questions to ask a classmate during an interview. Then interview that person.

MODEL: In your family, do you hug each other when you see each other?

Step 3. Prepare a set of statements in which you compare what your family does and what your partner's family does using the ideas from Steps 1 and 2. You will present these to the class and after everyone has offered ideas, you will draw some conclusions.

In Step 2, the first output phase, the learner is using only one form (in Spanish) in each question that he has to create. The learner isolates the one form and its function and then uses it to communicate something. In Step 3, the learner produces output again, but this time using the two forms from Steps 1 and 2.

Activities such as structured output may be useful for promoting output procedures and skill (fluency) if the learner is at the right stage. At any stage, however, structured output tasks serve another useful purpose. As learners create structured sentences to express meaning to someone else, their output becomes input for others. The stimulus sentences in Step 1 are also input in that they are read and their meaning must be comprehended for the activity to take place. In addition, such tasks do not normally occur without interaction with the instructor, who may follow up with questions and statements that also serve as input.

IMPLICATION 4: FOCUS ON FORM (OR GRAMMAR INSTRUCTION) SHOULD BE MEANING-BASED AND TIED TO INPUT OR COMMUNICATION

The days of drilling, filling in blanks with the correct verb form, transforming sentences, using slash sentences for practicing agreement, and performing other strictly form-focused tasks should be long gone. Although all these tasks are useful for filling time and textbook pages, it is clear from research that such activities do not promote acquisition. Concern for accuracy has been replaced by a concern for noticing things in the input. The term **input enhancement**, coined by Michael Sharwood Smith, probably captures best how teachers might direct efforts at getting learners to acquire formal aspects of language.

The idea behind input enhancement is simple: A **focus on form** should not take place in the absence of meaning. That is, a focus on form should happen in one of two ways: (1) through a communicative interchange or (2) through some kind of comprehension task. Focusing on form through communicative interchanges comes in a variety of shapes. **Recasts** are restatements by a speaker when a non-native speaker produces something that is not quite right. The speaker does not take the focus off meaning, but instead temporarily puts the focus on meaning *and* form. Here are two examples. The first is from a naturalistic conversation; the second is from a research report on the use of recasts to push acquisition along.

Exchange 1

NON-NATIVE SPEAKER: So he go to the store.
NATIVE SPEAKER: He went to the store, and then what happened?
NON-NATIVE SPEAKER: So he went to the store and, he, uh, he buy . . .

Exchange 2

PARTICIPANT: Maria toma café a veces.
RESEARCHER: Maria toma a veces café, ¿sí? uhuhm.

(Ortega & Long, 1997, p. 78)

In each case, the non-learner merely restated the learner's meaning in a correct way. Meaning was not lost since the learner is engaged in expressing some kind of meaning and the other person is simply providing help via a corrected version. The learner is not asked to repeat (that would not normally happen in a conversation!), but learners sometimes do rephrase what they say as they continue to speak.

The other main type of focus on form during a communicative act is the confirmation check. That is, a listener may query a learner about something just said to confirm the informational intent, which might lead to a negotiated "correct way" of saying what the learner wanted to say. These look like the interchange between Bob and Tom that we saw in Chapter 2.

Sometimes a listener simply might not understand what an L2 learner has said. This can lead to a clarification request. Different from recasts and confirmation checks, **clarification requests** are overt questions about what the learner is trying to say. They often involve questions such as "Do you mean. . . ?" or "What do you mean?", and sometimes something as simple as "Huh?" What the listener is signaling is noncomprehension, whereas recasts and confirmation checks indicate that something has been comprehended. In the following interchange, there is a pronunciation problem and the native speaker has to simply ask the learner what she means.

NON-NATIVE: And they have the chwach there.
    NATIVE: The what? (clarification request)
NON-NATIVE: The chwach—I know someone that—
    NATIVE: What does it mean? (an attempt to clarify again)
NON-NATIVE: Like, um, American people they always go there every Sunday.
    NATIVE: Yes? (said in such a way as to signal comprehension still not achieved)
NON-NATIVE: You know—every morning that there pr—that the American people get dressed up to got to, um, chwach.
    NATIVE: Oh, to church—I see.

(From Pica, 1987, cited in Gass & Selinker, 2001, p. 303)

The second way that a focus on form can occur—through some kind of comprehension task—is best illustrated by text enhancement and structured input. **Text enhancement** involves targeting a particular form or structure in a written text that the learners read for meaning (because they are going to discuss it, write something about it, and so on). The targeted item might be underlined throughout, put into boldface, or altered in some other way so that it "pops out" to the learner. The idea is that learners are more likely to notice something in the input if it is highlighted.

Structured input is part of a more elaborate approach to focus on form called *processing instruction.* As mentioned in Chapter 5, processing instruction consists of explanation regarding a structure or form, explanation about a possible processing problem (e.g., learners are told about the first-noun strategy), and activities involving structured input. In structured input tasks, learners respond to input sentences that are structured in such a way as to discourage an input-processing strategy that may not help them acquire something. For example, adverbs of time are removed from input sentences if the task is to process past tense; learners have to process object-verb-subject sentences correctly if the task is to avoid the first-noun strategy. In one kind of activity, called *referential,* learners indicate that they have processed the form by attaching it to its meaning. For example, they might hear a sentence such as "John talked on the phone" and have to indicate which adverb could go with it: "right now, yesterday, tomorrow." In affective activities, learners indicate opinions, beliefs, truth values, and so on. Continuing with the past tense, an instructor might put up a series of sentences on an overhead about what she did last night:

I . . .

  _____ prepared dinner.
  _____ had a cocktail.
  _____ read the newspaper.

_____ watched TV.

_____ walked the dog.

_____ called a friend on the phone.

_____ corrected papers.

_____ exercised.

Students are then instructed to first check off those they think she did, after which the instructor tells them if they are correct. Then the students are instructed to put the items in the order in which she did them. At no time do they actually produce the form or create past tense forms. (They may read the ones out loud on the overhead, but this is not output as defined in this book—that is, learners creating with language to express their own meaning.) Notice in this activity that there are no adverbs of time in the sentences and that the subject has been separated out at the top so that each verb form appears in initial position; structured input activities always keep in mind the learners' processing strategies.

These are just a handful of the various options available for focusing on form while keeping meaning in focus as well. Research is still in progress on these and other techniques; so far, overall, it is clear that a focus on form and meaning at the same time is better than a focus on form without a focus on meaning.

IMPLICATION 5: WE SHOULD WATCH OUT FOR WHAT WE EXPECT OF LEARNERS

This implication is perhaps the hardest one to consider when developing curricula and materials that foster acquisition. Basically, it means that we shouldn't expect learners to produce what they can't produce. In my capacity as a language program director, I have often observed well-meaning novice instructors ask beginning students the deadly question "Why?" after the students have provided a response to a *yes/no* question (e.g., Do you like cats? [No.] Why?). There is either silence or a halting attempt by the student to offer some kind of explanation. Learners simply can't speak in full sentences at this stage in any spontaneous way, even though they really want to and they like what they are talking about. Remember from Processability Theory's hierarchy of output procedures that these procedures require time to acquire and control.

More than one person has suggested that the initial stages of learning should be comprehension-oriented, that basic language courses should push students to their limits in understanding and interpreting language. Some have gone so far as to say students should be allowed to be silent in class if they choose, as long as they are actively listening. These proposals, whether practical or not, have merit for scrutiny in acquisition-oriented beginning classes. They focus our attention on the first critical process in acquisition: comprehension of input. Attempts to put such curricula into practice have met with varied success, but the research on them supports their success in *beginning*-level classes. However, a steady diet of comprehension only throughout one's language learning experience does not maximize acquisition, as we have seen. The idea here is that we shouldn't force beginners to talk very much until they've built up a developing system. Comprehension is also something that everyone can work on alone outside of class (taking individual differences into account).

Regardless of whether one adopts a comprehension-first curriculum, it is important to be sensitive to students' production abilities. Because speaking has always been the hallmark of acquisition ("Is she fluent in Chinese?"), there has been a tremendous push since World War II for language instruction to be production-oriented in some way or another. We should be mindful, however, that the goals of fluency and strong output abilities are end products of acquisition. The question to consider is this: Should production be the goal of every class hour we teach?

SUMMARY

In this Epilogue we posited five implications of SLA research for the development of L2 curricula. They are:

- the more input, the better (the more meaning-based the class, the better);
- the more interaction, the better;
- all learner production should be meaning-based or communicative;
- focus on form (or grammar instruction) should be meaning-based and tied to input or communication; and
- we should watch out for what we expect of learners.

In a sense, we have done for teaching in this chapter what we did for SLA in Chapter 1: We have put down some givens. That is, these implications can be considered givens for any curriculum that aims to develop acquisition (and communicative abilities as a co-product). To be sure, these givens are actually guidelines—and broad ones at that. However, broad guidelines can be useful in that they allow teachers to explore a range of options and to identify materials and practices that not only fit the guidelines but also fit their own teaching styles and contexts of learning.

FINAL COMMENT: BACK TO THE BEGINNING

Research on the effects of instruction on language acquisition is the subject for another book. From the glimpses offered in this book, it is clear that language teaching for acquisition is not always effective. Like acquisition itself, instructional effects are constrained. Instruction appears to be effective when it is directed toward acquisition processes or at least uses these processes to inform itself of what *should* be effective based on the research. This does not mean that SLA research has the answers to all possible questions about SLA. But language teachers should not be discouraged, for at least some things are clear. In this chapter we have attempted to distill some research results into a handful of statements around which teachers and curriculum developers can fashion instructional efforts. We end here by returning to where we started in the prologue: a quote from S. Pit Corder. With thirty-five years of research behind us, we can at least *begin* to do exactly what Corder envisioned:

We may be able to allow the learner's innate strategies to dictate our practice and determine our syllabus; we may learn to adapt ourselves to *his* needs rather than impose upon him *our* preconceptions of *how* he ought to learn, *what* he ought to learn and *when* he ought to learn it.

READ MORE ABOUT IT

Doughty, C., & Williams, J. (Eds.). (1998). *Focus on form in classroom second language acquisition*. Cambridge: Cambridge University Press.

Hinkel, E., & Fotos, S. (Eds.). (2002). *New perspectives on grammar teaching in second language classrooms*. Mahwah, NJ: Erlbaum.

Krashen, S. D., & Terrell, T. D. (1983). *The natural approach*. San Francisco: Alemany Press.

Lee, J. F. (2000). *Tasks and communicating in language classrooms*. New York: McGraw-Hill.

Lee, J. F., & VanPatten, B. (1995). *Making communicative language teaching happen*. New York: McGraw-Hill. [2nd ed., 2003.]

Nunan, D. (1989). *Designing tasks for the communicative classroom*. Cambridge: Cambridge University Press.

Ortega, L., & Long, M. H. (1997). The effects of models and recasts on the acquisition of object topicalization and adverb placement in L2 Spanish. *Spanish Applied Linguistics*, 1, 65–86.

Savignon, S. (1997). *Communicative competence: Theory and classroom practice*. New York: McGraw-Hill.

VanPatten, B. (1996). *Input processing and grammar instruction*. Norwood, NJ: Ablex.

VanPatten, B. (2002). Processing instruction: An update. *Language Learning*, 52, 755–803.

Winitz, H. (Ed.) (1981). *The comprehension approach to foreign language instruction*. Rowley, MA: Newbury House.

GLOSSARY

access: activation of lexical items (words) and grammatical forms in the developing system for the purpose of communicating particular meanings.

accommodation: the process by which the developing system accepts a new grammatical form or structure after it has been mapped onto meaning during input processing.

acoustic salience: the degree to which a word or form stands out in an utterance; two factors that affect acoustic salience are stress and position in the utterance.

acquisition: the sets of processes by which learners internalize a linguistic system; we can also talk about the acquisition of output-processing procedures separate from the linguistic system.

acquisition orders: the chronological order in which learners master certain grammatical forms as evidenced in their speech.

Audiolingual Method (ALM): a widespread language teaching method used in the late 1950s and 1960s that relied on memorization, repetition, and drilling.

automatization: the process by which a learner comes to perform a procedure without conscious thought or effort.

behaviorism: a field of psychology prevalent in the first half of the twentieth century that relied on a stimulus–response paradigm; an organism was said to learn by having particular behaviors rewarded.

clarification request: the use of language during a conversation to get the speaker to make adjustments so the listener can understand something he or she is not sure of or did not understand, e.g., "Did you mean . . . ?".

communication: the expression, interpretation, and negotiation of meaning in a given social and situational context.

communication strategy: any strategy used by a speaker to get an idea across or to express meaning.

confirmation check: language used by a listener during a conversation to make sure he or she understood what the speaker just said, e.g., "So she didn't leave, right?".

content words: words that carry significant meaning in the utterance, as opposed to words that may have a grammatical function and whose meaning may not be crucial to comprehension; sometimes called the "big" words.

content-based instruction: a type of learning experience in which subject matter (history, geography, the sciences, and so on) is taught in a second language.

context of learning: the situation in which a language is learned; determined by whether there is classroom experience and whether the language is the language spoken in the geographic location of learning (see **foreign language** and **second language**).

Critical Period Hypothesis: the idea that a second language is more difficult to acquire or impossible to acquire completely after a particular age, usually said to be puberty.

declarative knowledge: information about how something works or how to do something.

developing system: the complex and evolving linguistic system in the mind or brain of the second language learner.

developmental stages: the steps exhibited by learners as they slowly acquire a particular structure, such as negation, word order, or question formation.

discourse competence: the underlying knowledge of cohesion and coherence; the knowledge of how sentences and utterances go together to make a whole, either in written language or in spoken language.

event probabilities: the degree to which one situation is more plausible or more frequent than another, e.g., the event of a parent spanking a child is more probable than that of a child spanking a parent, even though either is capable of performing the act of spanking.

explicit knowledge/explicit rules: conscious knowledge of rules usually developed under explicit conditions, such as teaching and practicing; the learner is able to articulate the rule in some way.

external factors: factors from the environment that influence learning, e.g., the quality and quantity of input or interactions with others.

fluency: the degree to which a person can speak effortlessly and without much error.

focus on form: the act of drawing learners' attention to a formal feature of language.

foreign language context: the context in which the language being learned is not spoken outside the classroom (in the geographic location of learning).

foreigner talk: simplified and sometimes ungrammatical speech used with nonnatives who are perceived to have very limited second language ability.

formal relationship: a relationship in which two items in the lexical-form network are linked because of a matching formal feature, e.g., *unnerving* and *unsettling* are linked because of the prefix as well as the suffix.

form–meaning connection: the mapping that a learner makes between a formal feature of language and its real-world referent, e.g., that *–ed* means past.

fossilization: the process by which a learner plateaus or stops learning; this process can happen to part of the developing system or the entire system.

grammaticality judgments: tests given to native speakers or to learners in which they must determine whether a sentence is permissible (possible) in the language being learned; the determination is made by reference to structural aspects rather than meaning.

immersion: the context in which a learner acquires the language when living, working, or going to school where that language is used.

implicational hierarchy: in linguistics, a hierarchy in which one structure in a language implies that the language has other related structures; in acquisition, a hierarchy in which one acquired structure or form suggests that another or other structures must already be acquired as well.

implicit linguistic system: the learner's linguistic system that exists outside of consciousness.

indirect correction: indication of a learner's error via normal conversational behaviors, such as clarification requests, confirmation checks, recasts, and others.

individual differences: the collection of strategies and behaviors in explicit learning situations that distinguish people from each other.

input: the communicative language a learner hears or reads in context and to which he or she attends for its meaning.

input enhancement: any manner in which formal features of the language are brought to the learner's attention by an instructor.

input processing: the stage of acquisition when learners first make form–meaning connections and parse sentences during the act of comprehension.

intake: linguistic data held in working memory and made available for further processing; the result of input processing.

interaction: conversational exchange involving two or more persons.

internal factors: cognitive and linguistic factors that the learner brings to the task of learning another language; these include but are not limited to processing constraints and strategies, prior linguistic knowledge (e.g., knowledge of other languages), predispositions toward language as a result of universal grammar, and the general "architecture" of the brain or mind.

lexical relationship: a relationship in which two items in the lexical-form network are linked because of a matching root, e.g., *unnerving* and *nervous* are linked because of the root *nerv*.

lexical semantics: the meaning underlying a verb that requires the subject to be of a certain type, e.g., for the verb *kick* the requirements are that the noun be animate and have a foot, hoof, or other similar appendage to kick with.

lexicon: all the words a learner knows that are stored in the developing system.

limited capacity: the constraints on working memory in terms of size and processing space.

modification (of input): any change in input by a speaker that results in elaboration or alteration of an utterance because the learner did not understand the sentence initially.

monitoring: the process by which a speaker is aware of how he or she is saying something with the idea of editing it if the need arises.

morphology: the structure of words involving inflections, prefixes, and suffixes.

Natural Approach: an instructional type that uses only the L2 and attempts to provide as much input in the classroom as possible.

network of forms and lexical items: the weblike subsystem in the developing system that contains all the words the learner knows as well as links between them and formal features.

output: language the learner produces to communicate or express a meaning.

output processing: the manner in which learners (or any speakers) string together words and formal features of language to create utterances; it involves two main processes, access and production-based strategies.

overt correction: indication of a learner's error by drawing the learner's attention to it, such as by saying, "No, say it this way" or "You just made an error. You mean . . .".

parameters: the various options of a particular abstract syntactic property or rule; some languages set a parameter one way and others set it another way.

parsing: the projection of a syntactic structure onto a sentence as one is engaged in comprehension.

phonology: the structure of sounds.

possible sentence/structure: a structure or rule that is allowed in a language and that results in a possible sentence; e.g., subject-verb inversion is not allowed in English, so *Ate John his breakfast?* is not a possible sentence, while it is a possible sentence in Spanish, Italian, and other languages.

pragmatics: knowledge of what a speaker's intent is when the meaning intended does not match the sentence structure.

prefabricated patterns: parts of sentences that learners store as whole chunks that can be combined with other units to make utterances, e.g., *Whatsa*.

procedural knowledge: knowledge that underlies how to do something, said to normally follow declarative knowledge in skill-building theory.

processing instruction: a type of focus on form that is informed by input processing; it attempts to alter or modify learners' processing strategies to improve intake.

production strategies: the procedures that are used by the output mechanisms to create utterances and that exist in an implicational hierarchy.

recast: a restatement of what a person says during a communicative interaction.

redundancy: the expression of meaning by both a formal feature of language and a content word in a sentence.

restructuring: the process by which parts of the developing system change as the result of the accommodation of a new form or structure.

routines: utterances stored in the learner's developing system as whole chunks, e.g., *Idunno*.

second language: any language that is not a native language, including a foreign language.

second language acquisition (SLA): the creation of a linguistic system in the mind/brain of someone who speaks another language; this is different from second language acquisition *use*, that is, the use of a second language for communicative purposes.

second language context: the context in which the language being learned is spoken outside the classroom (in the geographic location of learning).

semantic processing: input processing in which learners attend only to the meaning of utterances and not necessarily to how the meaning was expressed.

semantic relationship: a relationship in which words in the developing system are linked based on meaning, e.g., the words *uninteresting* and *boring* are linked via meaning.

simplification (of input): the act of making input less complex by reducing clause structure, shortening sentences, and other means.

skill: the ability to perform some act.

sociolinguistics: underlying knowledge about appropriateness of language use.

speaker's intent: what a speaker means by an utterance regardless of what the structure of that utterance is; e.g., not all questions require an answer, since some can be rhetorical questions and some can be meant as commands.

structured input: the type of manipulated input used in processing instruction; the input pushes learners away from nonoptimal processing strategies.

structured output: the type of speech produced by learners performing a communicative task that requires a particular grammatical form or structure.

syntactic processing: input processing in which learners attend not only to the meaning of an utterance but also to how that meaning is encoded linguistically.

syntax: the structure of sentences and the abstract rules that govern the structure.

teacher talk: simplified input as used by instructors in language classes.

text enhancement: the highlighting of grammatical forms in a written text to increase their salience.

transfer: the reliance on the first language for the creation of the developing system.

working memory: the processing and storage space in the mind or brain in which language computations are carried out during comprehension on a millisecond-by-millisecond basis.

GENERAL REFERENCES

This list contains readings not found at the ends of chapters. The list is not meant to be exhaustive but suggestive. In addition, the list contains some works that may seem out of date to some scholars but yet contain the basis upon which current research is being produced. And I've sprinkled in a few items on child L1 acquisition as well as on language in general in case you'd like to browse those areas. As with most articles and books, the references contained in each work will lead the reader to other sources.

Byrnes, H. (1998). *Learning foreign and second languages: Perspectives in research and scholarship*. New York: Modern Language Association of America.

Brown, G., Malmaker, K., & Williams, J. (Eds.). (1996). *Performance and competence in second language acquisition*. Cambridge: Cambridge University Press.

Chaudron, C. (1988). *Second language classrooms: Research on teaching and learning*. Cambridge: Cambridge University Press.

Cook, V. (1991). *Second language learning and language teaching*. London: Edward Arnold.

Crain, S., & Lillo-Martin, D. (1999). *An introduction to linguistic theory and language acquisition*. Oxford: Blackwell.

Day, R. (Ed.). (1986). *Talking to learn: Conversations in second language acquisition*. Rowley, MA: Newbury House.

Eckman, F. R., Highland, D., Lee, P. W., Mileham, J., & Rutkowski Weber, R. (Eds.). (1995). *Second language acquisition theory and pedagogy*. Mahwah, NJ: Erlbaum.

Ellis, R. (1994). *The study of second language acquisition*. Oxford: Oxford University Press.

Freed, B. (Ed.). (1991). *Foreign language acquisition research and the classroom*. Lexington, MA: D. C. Heath.

Gass, S. M., & Madden, C. (Eds.). (1985). *Input in second language acquisition*. Rowley, MA: Newbury House.

Gass, S. M., & Selinker, L. (2001). *Second language acquisition: An introductory course*. Mahwah, NJ: Erlbaum.

Gleitman, L. R., & Liberman, M. (Eds.). (1995). *Language*. Cambridge, MA: MIT Press. [This book is part of a series titled *An Invitation to Cognitive Science*.]

Ingram, D. (1989). *First language acquisition: Method, description and explanation*. Cambridge: Cambridge University Press.

Krashen, S. D. (1982). *Principles and practice in second language acquisition*. London: Pergamon.

Lantolf, J. P., & Appel, G. (Eds.). (1994). *Vygotskian approaches to second language research.* Norwood, NJ: Ablex.

Markee, N. (2000). *Conversation analysis.* Mahwah, NJ: Erlbaum.

Musumeci, D. (1997). *Breaking tradition: An exploration of the historical relationship between theory and practice in second language teaching.* New York: McGraw-Hill.

Newmeyer, F. J. (Ed.). (1988). *Language: Psychological and biological aspects.* Cambridge: Cambridge University Press. [This book is part of a series titled *Linguistics: The Cambridge Survey.*]

Pinker, S. (1994). *The language instinct.* New York: Morrow.

Schmidt, R. (Ed.). (1995). *Attention and awareness in foreign language learning.* Honolulu: University of Hawaii.

Schumann, J. H. (1978). *The pidginization process: A model for language acquisition.* Rowley, MA: Newbury House.

Selinker, L. (1992). *Rediscovering interlanguage.* London: Longman.

Skehan, P. (1998). *A cognitive approach to language learning.* Oxford: Oxford University Press.

Towell, R., & Hawkins, R. (1994). *Approaches to second language acquisition.* Clevedon, UK: Multilingual Matters.

Index